GRIEF IN
CHILDREN

GRIEF IN CHILDREN

SECOND EDITION

A HANDBOOK FOR ADULTS

ATLE DYREGROV

FOREWORD BY PROFESSOR WILLIAM YULE

Jessica Kingsley Publishers
London and Philadelphia

First published as *Sorg hos Barn: En Håndbok for Voksne* in Norway in 1990
First published in English in the United Kingdom in 1991
by Jessica Kingsley Publishers
116 Pentonville Road
London N1 9JB, UK
and
400 Market Street, Suite 400
Philadelphia, PA 19106, USA

www.jkp.com

Library of Congress Cataloging in Publication Data
Dyregrov, Atle.
  Grief in children : a handbook for adults / Atle Dyregrov ; foreword by William Yule. -- 2nd ed.
    p. cm.
  Includes bibliographical references.
  ISBN 978-1-84310-612-8 (pb : alk. paper) 1. Grief in children. 2. Children and death. I.
Title.
  BF723.G75D97 2008
  155.9'37083--dc22
                                                           2007040139

British Library Cataloguing in Publication Data
A CIP catalogue record for this book is available from the British Library

ISBN 978 1 84310 612 8

Printed and bound in Great Britain by
Athenaeum Press, Gateshead, Tyne and Wear

Contents

Foreword

There is still a strong tendency in many Western countries to try to protect young children from many of the unpleasant or difficult aspects of life, rather than to prepare children to understand and cope with these. Death and bereavement are just such issues. At first sight, there are huge differences between cultures as to how these are dealt with. Even within a single country, different subgroups approach the topics in vastly differing ways.

Police officers often have the task of breaking the news about a death to a family. When I first started working with the family liaison officers of the Metropolitan Police in London a few years ago, many reported that the most difficult thing was knowing how to tell a child that a parent had died. The impulse to shield children from bad news was getting in the way of helping the child and family. In discussions, my colleague and I established that there were great differences in expectations over, for example, whether a child should attend a funeral or view the dead body. Initial views were forcefully expressed – until it became evident that within the group there were many differing, equally strongly held views. It often boiled down to accepting that what one had experienced oneself as a child was not the only way of doing things.

Brief reflection made it clear that in some parts of the country or in some religions, children were encouraged to view bodies whilst in other groups such activity was taboo; some children participated in funerals whilst in other cases they were banned from attending. What guidance could an officer give a family in times of crisis?

Similarly, teachers can be faced with the difficult task of explaining to a group of children why a classmate will not be returning. Teachers cannot hide behind the published research and say 'Johnny is not here but a meta-analysis says I must not discuss this with you for at least six weeks'! Rather, the concerned class teacher has to find appropriate ways of both explaining what has happened to the children and then helping them cope with their reactions to the news.

And, of course, parents often need advice in how best to deal with children's reactions, particularly after a sudden death. Where there has been a chronic illness, usually people are partly prepared to help children face the death, but the parents themselves will also be grieving and this can make for complications.

I recently was consulted by the mother of a ten-year-old boy who has Asperger's Syndrome. The boy had a strong attachment to his father, but the father died unexpectedly in an accident. The mother – a considered agnostic – was shocked to find herself telling her son that his father had gone to heaven to be with the angels. 'Where is heaven?', came the first question. 'Above the clouds' was her reply. Then, when the remaining family flew off on holiday, the boy's piercing voice was heard above the noise of the jets – 'Mummy. There's the clouds, but I cannot see Daddy'.

Equally unprepared were the many families in Sri Lanka bereaved by the sudden tsunami. Having worked there for many years, I responded to an invitation to go a few weeks after the tsunami struck. My colleagues and I found we were asked for advice about bereavement much more than about traumatic stress disorders in the first few weeks. Many stunned parents told their children that their other parent had gone overseas to work, rather than tell them the truth – even where the child had been on the beach with the dead parent when the giant wave struck. Even many experienced teachers felt that children under the age of ten should not be told about death.

With sudden death likely to happen at any time, it seems obvious to me that teachers, police, health workers and parents should all have some preparation for how to react should the dreaded event happen. Different groups will require different levels of preparation, but all will benefit from a better understanding of how children of different ages understand death and how they react to bereavement.

And this is where this marvellous book has an important part to play. For years, I have strongly advised these adults to read 'Grief in Children' because I believe it is the most sympathetically written and accessible book on the topic. It is the thoughtful distillation of many years' clinical experience of working with bereaved children and their families. Atle Dyregrov has listened to what the children have said and to what they have said they need to help them. Moreover, the suggestions and advice are tempered with an encyclopaedic knowledge of the most up-to-date research in the area.

This second edition of the book includes many more vignettes describing children's questions and reactions. It incorporates more material on traumatic deaths resulting in complicated grieving that may require expert help. Recent studies on suicide and its effects on surviving children extend

Introduction

There is a lot of potential for children to experience death. Parents, grandparents, siblings, friends, friends' parents, teachers or other known adults or children may die. When younger people die, this hits both adults and children especially hard. The number of children who experience the death of a loved one is very considerable.

Many deaths happen suddenly, in dramatic ways. There has been an increase in murder, suicide and accidental death in modern society. But a death after a cardiac arrest may also be sudden, unanticipated and dramatic. We know that sudden deaths often have more serious consequences both physically and mentally. This book will address sudden death in more depth than anticipated death. Sudden and dramatic deaths create more anxiety and other reactions, which are difficult to face at home or in school. If a death involves a child, the death has the potential to cause repercussions in the peer group, the school or the play group. Man-made and natural disasters often affect large groups of people, and may cause several deaths within communities. Such events almost always leave a trail of grief in the child community.

Schools and play groups will be affected in different ways by death. Whether it is children, parents of school- or play group-children, or teachers who die, the need for information about children's reactions and helpful ways of handling the situation is necessary to understand and care for children. Children have a great capacity for coping with difficult situations if the adult recovery environment can provide them with insight and understanding.

To be able to help children in grief you have to understand children at different age levels, their concepts, grief reactions and potential symptoms. You also need to know how you can help the child. This book will, it is hoped, give the reader a fundament of knowledge about children's grief reactions and how they can be helped. But it is important to remember that, although one may have the necessary knowledge, this will be of little help if the person using this knowledge does not provide it within a caring, empathic relationship.

Chapter One

Children's reactions to grief and crisis

Children's understanding of death at different ages

Children's understanding of death develops in parallel with the child's cognitive maturing through childhood. The development of the concept of death may occur at slightly different rates, but the developmental sequence seems to be the same.

Below the age of five

Children younger than five do not understand that death is final, and will clearly demonstrate this in how they speak about it:

> 'Can't we help Papa up from his grave?'
> 'When will my baby sister come back?'

Their maturity does not allow an understanding of how the body and its parts function. Death is reversible for them, and they do not fathom that all the functions of life have ceased. That someone is gone forever is beyond their grasp:

> 'Who will give the baby milk up in heaven?'
> 'Couldn't we bring some lemonade for Papa in his grave?'
> 'Can she listen through all that soil?'

The questions reflect young children's concern about the physical well-being of the dead person: how they get food, if they are warm, and so forth. They do not have an understanding of death as universal, happening to everybody:

'Can boy babies also die?'

Small children are able to use the word *death* without understanding the full meaning of the word. At this stage a child will have difficulty understanding abstract explanations of death. A four-year-old child who is told that her mother is in heaven, and at the same time told that she is buried in her grave, can easily experience confusion:

'Where can we take the bus to Jesus?'
'Where is the ladder?'

Children think in very concrete terms at this age, and it is best to refrain from abstract explanations, or euphemisms that a child might take quite literally, such as saying that the dead person is asleep or gone on a long journey. It is not uncommon to see a child to whom death has been explained in this manner afraid when his or her parents are taking an afternoon nap, or sharply protesting if somebody is leaving on a journey. If sleep is used as an explanation, a child might think that 'If I make a lot of noise, she will wake up.'

Children are very sensitive to separations, and this is increased when euphemisms are used. Even short separations can be experienced as permanent loss by children, as their time sense is not fully developed.

Even though smaller children's concept of death is not fully developed, there is no reason to doubt that they react strongly to loss at this age. Even children less than two years old are able to express their understanding that someone is not present any more, and remember this for a long time afterwards:

John, at one and a half years old, had a sister who died in sudden infant death syndrome (SIDS). In the period following the loss he went to her bed and said: 'Ba [baby]?' in a questioning tone. Some months afterwards the bed was prepared for a visiting child. Again John went to the bed, put his head among the blankets, and said: 'Ba?'

The youngest children can, as a result of their pre-logical thinking, have misconceptions about what causes a death:

'If you hadn't gone to the clinic (delivery room), the baby wouldn't have died.'

During the preschool years children conceive of time as somehow circular. Their daily routines are made up of things that are repeated: they get up, go through the day, go to bed, fall asleep and the next day this is repeated. No wonder they think that first one is small, then one grows big, and then small again. Many things repeat themselves, and children experience time as moving in a circle. So also with death: we live, we die and then we live again.

From the perspective of child psychology it is held that children are partly dominated by 'magical thinking', where they experience themselves as the centre of things. Therefore, they may believe that their thoughts, feelings, wishes and actions can cause what happens to them and others. Maybe this is more true in theory than in real life, but it should be remembered that such thinking can make a child think that he or she caused the death. Maybe it is these magical qualities that show up when they think that the deceased can be returned to life.

The young child's lack of understanding of a death's more far-reaching consequences explains some of the lack of reaction that the child may show upon learning of an event. Parents have reported that their child said 'Can I go out and play now?' shortly after they have been told of their mother or father's sudden death. Later in the day they come and ask: 'When is Mama coming?'

Children of preschool age also differentiate feelings to a lesser degree than older children and they have less experience in regulating and reducing their feelings. They may say that they are 'very, very, very sad', using the adjective 'very' several times to describe a feeling, rather than introducing another adjective.

Even though a child's age and maturity sets clear limits for an acceleration of their understanding of death, small children's understanding can be influenced by a concrete meeting with death, leading to a more mature understanding than their peers:

> Sean (aged four and a half) lost his best friend in an accident. Before accompanying his parents to a viewing of his friend he showed his immature understanding (or lack of experience) by saying: 'In 14 days he will be back', 'When the summer holiday is over, he will be back'. On his way home from this event he expressed a more mature view by stating: 'Now we can never go bathing together', 'Now we cannot play with the tools any more'.

Between four and six years of age, children gradually develop a biological, more than psychological, understanding of what life is. While a small child can think that a heart is there to love someone, the lungs to speak and the stomach to eat, children in or approaching school age will understand that the body, and its parts, all have one common goal; to sustain life (Slaughter 2005). When this more complex understanding of the body and its organs have developed, there is a better basis for understanding what will happen if the body's organs fail or are damaged.

From five to ten

Children in the age-range from five to ten years old gradually develop an understanding of death as irreversible, with all life functions ended: 'when you are dead, you are dead'. Around the age of seven children seem to get a better grip on, and understanding of, death as unavoidable and universal. But they are still resistant to thinking of death as a possibility for themselves. In the same way as younger children, they are concrete in their thinking, and they need concrete expressions (rituals, pictures, tombstone) as support for their grief work. Their understanding of the causes of death is also concrete. They can both understand death as a result of external causes, such as accidents and violence, and as a result of inner processes, such as disease and old age. Their interest may start to centre on the process of dying and decomposition and what caused the death. Magical components are still part of their thinking; they may assume that the dead person can see or hear the living, and they may work hard to please the deceased as a consequence of this.

During this age-span children see themselves less as the centre of the universe, and their ability to comprehend the perspective of others is increased. They therefore feel more compassion towards friends who lose parents or siblings, as well as their own family members. Children are able to show empathic feelings at an early age (Raundalen 1989). As children grow older, they understand more of the cause and effect behind events, and they become more occupied with the justice and injustice of things that happen – that 'bad' things happen to 'good people': 'It was not fair that this should happen to her, she was always so nice.' Many children cope best with such events when they are given detailed information about the different aspects of the event.

Already in the preschool age, but more markedly in the early school-age, there seems to be a shift in children's willingness to express their feelings. Boys, especially, may start to suppress their feelings, in parallel with the learning that takes place within peer-groups and through observation and direct learning from adults (e.g. 'Big boys don't cry'). Parents may have the experience that their child keeps his or her grief to him- or herself, and is not willing to talk about what happened.

From ten through adolescence

From ten years of age children's concept of death becomes more abstract, and they are able to understand more of the long-term consequences of a loss. At this age they reflect even more on justice and injustice, fate and parapsychological (occult) phenomena. Together with the biological, psychological and social changes that take place, deaths that happen at this age can result in relatively strong reactions. Even though children at this age are able to conceive of death as an abstract idea, the understanding of death as universal and inevitable also means that it will be personal, with the need that this may create for keeping this thought at a distance.

During adolescence the ability to think hypothetically develops, in a way that makes it possible for children to view many aspects of an event. They are more able to draw parallels, and they can review inconsistencies in the information they receive about an event more critically. Cognitively they are more capable of reflecting on deeper themes and more existential aspects of death:

> Axel (15) lost his older brother in an accident. He was very sad over a prolonged period of time, especially when reflecting on all the things he knew that his brother never would experience, among these watching his own son grow up. His ability to use a future perspective made him reflect on what his brother would lose out on and what he himself never

would experience in relation to his brother. He used time on thinking on why this happened to his brother and him, and why this would happen to someone as kind as his brother. He was also able to express how strongly he felt the loss of a role model who had always been there for him and he understood how this loss could cast shadows over the rest of his life.

Although the development of children's understanding of death has been linked to their general cognitive development, it also seems to reflect their experience of death and dying. If a child experiences death at close hand, and is given explanations concerning the facts surrounding the death, he or she is likely to grasp these facts of life more readily than other children.

Those who wish to have a more thorough and detailed introduction to children's understanding of death at different stages are referred to Corr and Corr (1996) and Slaughter (2005).

Although we have limited knowledge about children's understanding of death across cultures, research indicates that there are few differences in what age children from different parts of the world understand what death involves (Cuddy-Casey and Orvaschel 1997). There are greater differences in how open and directly children are informed about a death and its causes, and how much they are involved in viewing a body and burials. Through work with children in different parts of the world in relation to war and disasters I have experienced a gradual change across cultures where a more open and direct communication with children about serious issues have become more common. This development is associated with favourable outcomes for children (Dyregrov 2001a). More information about cultural issues related to grief can be found in Parkes, Laungani and Young (1997).

Immediate grief reactions in children

When a death is anticipated, children's reactions reflect the way they are told about the possibility of death as it progresses. Mental preparation and their opportunity to bid farewell will help them in their anticipatory grief work (grief resulting from the knowledge that a death is likely to occur in the near future), and lead to a less intensive shock reaction when the death occurs than is possible following a sudden death. But, even given time for 'mental preparation', most deaths will cause immediate grief reactions in children.

Children, as adults, do not react in *one* way. There is a wide variation in how they react to the news that someone is dead.

The most common immediate reactions are:

- shock and disbelief
- dismay and protest
- apathy and being stunned
- continuation of usual activities.

Shock and disbelief

Shock and disbelief is evident when children say: 'It can't be true', 'You are wrong, I don't believe you' and so forth. Older children especially react in this way, and may feel quite numb as a consequence of what has happened. Children may refuse to accept the death and firmly maintain this – thus keeping the painful fact at a distance. Parents can be astonished that their children do not react more than they do:

> 'Over and over I went through in my mind what to say, and I expected an enormous reaction, and then she almost did not react. She had some questions, but was then as smiling as ever. Later her reactions were stronger.'

When children do not immediately react with strong feelings, this can confuse parents and other adults. They become concerned about the fact that their children do not cry. But this is a normal shock reaction, also typical among adults. What has happened has to be taken in step by step, and this mechanism helps to prevent the child becoming emotionally overwhelmed. It is a necessary and helpful protection mechanism that helps us to cope with extreme situations.

Dismay and protest

Some children immediately react with dismay and protest, and can be quite inconsolable:

> A ten-year-old girl learnt about her mother's sudden death and cried and cried for almost 20 minutes. Then she stopped to ask how it had happened, before she started crying again. Gradually she became calmer, started to plan for the rest of the day, but at the same time wanted more information about the circumstances surrounding the death. During the first period of days, crying spells came intermittently.

Other reactions

Other children can be more *apathetic, almost as though their feelings are stunned.* Quite a few will *continue almost as if nothing has happened* (e.g. 'Can I go out and play now?'), as if some kind of auto-pilot is in action. Children's ability to regulate emotions is under development and a dear person's death can be so powerful that it may be necessary to put on the 'brakes'. In the evening a child may say: 'Why isn't Daddy here?' When the world becomes chaotic and unsafe, it may feel secure to continue with ordinary and well-known activities, even though it might provoke the adults that might have expected quite a different reaction:

A girl of 11 shocked her surroundings by asking if she could go and sleep at her best friend's house shortly after she was informed about her mother's death. The information to her adult caretakers about how this most probably was the girl's way of forcing normality into a situation where her life was turned on its head made them allow the visit, instead of telling her that this was inappropriate behaviour. Her friend's family was contacted and told what had happened and she was allowed to return home early if necessary.

Usual grief reactions among children

Some of the most common grief reactions in children are:

- anxiety
- vivid memories
- sleep difficulties
- sadness and longing
- anger and acting-out behaviour
- guilt, self-reproach and shame
- school problems
- physical complaints.

Anxiety

Anxiety is a very common reaction in children following the death of a loved one. When somebody close to them dies, their sense of security in the world is badly shaken: 'If it happened to Dad, it can happen to you [Mama].' My experience is that the children's anxiety centres to a high degree on fear that something may happen to their parents (surviving parent or carer). They fear this more than they fear that something might happen to themselves. Thoughts of their own mortality become more common in adolescence (see the section on children's understanding of death).

The reactions of fear and anxiety take many forms. Smaller children become more clinging and demanding. They want to be close to their parents, and may react strongly to separations. Through comments and questions children may show that they harbour concerns that something may happen to their parents or remaining parent: 'If you die, will you get the grave beside Daddy's?', 'If you die while you are sleeping, what do we do then?' Older children display a somewhat more advanced expression of this fear: 'Must children pay parents' loans and mortgages if they die?' This last question reflects fear related to primary needs: 'Who will provide for me if something happens?' Another related example: 'When Papa has been ill for so long, will he get his wages?'

The fear for parents is intensified if they become ill, especially if the symptoms are similar to those of the dead person before they died. Sometimes children want to stop going to school:

> A 12-year-old boy lost his father as a result of cancer. He started being absent from school. From the information that the mother provided, it was clear that these absences came when the mother felt exhausted, tired and had headaches. His father's illness had started with similar complaints, and the boy feared that his mother might also become seriously ill. After the boy was given more information and assurances ('I am not sick, only tired') that these 'symptoms' were not a sign that his mother had cancer, his truancy ceased.

Children may also develop the fear of dying themselves. After his baby sister died, a three-year-old said: 'I do not want to die.' Children's fear is often evident at bedtime, and can markedly prolong this situation. They may become afraid of sleeping alone, want to sleep with their parents, demand that one of the parents should stay with them until they fall asleep, want the light on or the door open. They may also resist being alone at their home or returning to an empty home. Increased separation anxiety can result in protest at staying with others, including their grandparents.

Some children become jumpy following a death. This is more common when the death is sudden and dramatic, and is caused more by the trauma than the loss. Children develop an increased preparedness for danger, and are on the watch for new things to happen. They jump at sudden noises, or other sudden changes in their environment:

> A boy of nine pulled his covers over his head when he was going to sleep. He breathed through a small opening along the side. He feared he would be kidnapped and when he slept like this he believed the kidnappers would not see him.

This preparedness for danger (hypersensitivity) can, if it persists, lead to headaches, muscle tension and pain, and will almost always result in concentration difficulties and memory problems. Children who witness a death can develop such strong post-traumatic stress reactions that they qualify for what is called a post-traumatic stress disorder (PTSD). Such reactions will often lead to school problems. Traumatic reactions are more fully described in Dyregrov and Yule (2006).

Some children develop phobic behaviour following a death, especially if they witnessed what happened or found the body of the dead one. They do not want to hear the event mentioned, they avoid memories, and they avoid or refuse to go near the scene of the event. They may even avoid contact with friends or others present when the event occurred or when the body was found. In this manner they try to avoid the strong feelings that such reminders can trigger. Such behaviour can also reflect magical conceptions such as:

'If we talk about what happened, another accident might happen.'

The fear of a new death may also be evident in their demand for reassurance from parents that they will be careful. If it was a young sibling who died they may watch out for their mother during a new pregnancy, and show great concern that something shall not happen to the new baby. Sometimes children do not dare to become too attached to their new sibling, as if guarding themselves from a repetition of the pain.

Vivid memories

Vivid memories or images can fasten in 'the back of children's minds'. In crisis situations there is a kind of 'super memory', different from the ordinary memory. There seems to be a form of altered state of consciousness in which sensory impressions are registered, processed and memorized in a manner different from the ordinary. Images can fasten in all senses, and form strong memories. If children are witnesses to accidental death or they come upon the body of the dead, these images can be fastened on as an 'inner video'. Later, these images come back in the form of recollections or repeated intrusive images. In addition to visual impressions, detailed auditory, gustatory and tactile impressions can become intrusive:

> When her father fell to the floor at home and died of a heart attack, a teenage daughter complained of hearing the 'thump' and later she was very upset if anyone lost something on the floor and the sound reminded her of her father's fall.

Even before they master the language to express such experiences, children can carry such events in a non-verbal form, and then, when mastering language, give words to their impressions. Kaplow *et al.* (2006) describe a case of a girl who was 19 months old and in her mother's arms when the mother was shot by her husband (the father of the child). At the age of 11 the girl began to exhibit severe symptoms of PTSD in response to a traumatic reminder. Apparently the event resided outside of conscious or explicit memory, but was kept in implicit memory. Although explicit memory is closely linked to language systems, implicit memory stores emotional information that helps us survive in the face of threat (LeDoux 1998).

Sometimes 'memories' are produced in fantasy, and then replayed as an intrusive 'memory':

> A teenager told how he had had an image of how his brother had been killed. This fantasy picture repeated itself many times daily, and disturbed his concentration both at school and at home.

> A boy of 11 who had a brother who drowned was intensely bothered by fantasies in which he saw his brother fighting for his life in the water.

Memories or recollections can be triggered by direct and indirect reminders of the event. Recollections are usually strongest in the evening, and can cause problems in falling asleep. The memories may also take the form of dreams or nightmares.

Often the child uses different activities to avoid such unwelcome, repeated thoughts and images. Restlessness and uneasiness can therefore be a direct result of trying to master unwelcome recollections.

Sleep difficulties

Sleep difficulties, both in the form of difficulty in falling asleep and interruption of sleep, are common among children in grief. If the word *sleep* has been used to describe death, children may become afraid of sleeping and be very alert when their parents are sleeping. Difficulty in sleeping is related to increased anxiety and more time to think about what has happened after they have gone to bed. If strong recollections of the death are present, these have a tendency to appear more commonly in the evening when the child's thoughts are not occupied by other things. Fear activates the body and makes it difficult to sleep.

Waking up from bad dreams or nightmares is not uncommon. Children can even develop fear of dreams that repeat themselves, and therefore resist falling asleep. They may demand to sleep with their parent, caretaker or sibling. My experience is that children who are not given time to process (i.e. talk about, play, think about) a trauma during daytime, or who actively try to keep thoughts about what happened away, are more bothered by dreams and nightmares than those who are given the chance to confront what has happened.

Sadness and longing

Sadness and longing appear in different ways. Some children cry frequently over the loss of their loved one, and can, at times, be quite inconsolable. But younger children in particular have a short sadness-span and are usually not sad for long periods at a time. But sadness may also appear in different forms. The child may isolate him- or herself, withdraw or become more closed. Children may also hide their sadness so as not to make their parents sad. Sometimes when they cry they say that they are not crying over the loss, but for some other reason:

> Elise, four years old, would spend long periods of time in front of her dead baby sister's picture. Now and then when she was very sad, she cried, but would not admit that it was

her sister she cried for. She said it was because of things like
having headaches or a pain in her leg, or that she had
nothing to do.

Longing encompasses everything from the daily hugs and the
security that being with the deceased provided, to help with
homework, driving to various activities and so forth. Sadness
and longing are felt even more severely when viewing other
people's happiness; for example, seeing other children with
their mother or father when they do not have both any more,
or when they see others with a pram when they have just lost a
baby brother or sister:

> Solveig lost her father when she was two and a half. When
> she approached 11 she thought more and more about the
> fact that she had no father. When her friends were driven to
> handball training by their fathers, she felt it almost unbear-
> ably hard. Other activities where it would have been natural
> that her father would have been present also reminded her
> of her loss and could lead to sadness and longing. She grad-
> ually improved as she learnt methods that helped her to
> distract and stop the thoughts that triggered her longing,
> parallel with setting aside a specific time to think of and
> write about her dad once a week.

The *longing for the lost one* may also appear as:

- searching for the lost one
- preoccupation with memories
- feeling the dead person's presence
- identification with the dead.

Smaller children may go from room to room and look for the
one who is dead. *Searching for the dead* is also reflected in children's need to talk about the deceased, or by expecting to see
or meet him or her. They may seek out places they used to

visit together, or engage in the same activities they used to do, to feel a sense of being close to the dead person. Sometimes they can set out on a more goal-directed search for the dead:

> A six-year-old girl set out several times, without any warning, for the churchyard where her 12-year-old sister was buried. Her parents would find her there without proper clothing, in all kinds of weather. In play therapy she was preoccupied with graveyards and burial rituals. For a period her favourite play was to bury a 'dead' crocodile. She did this over and over again. When the crocodile was buried, she would give words to the feelings that the 'grieving' crocodiles experienced when they visited the grave. Her parents had kept information from her, so as not to upset her. Through her play she sought to get a better understanding of what had happened, and the play brought her at the same time closer to her sister and provided an opportunity to give words to feelings.

Preoccupation with memories can also help in easing the loss. Children sometimes, to the distress of adults, wish to look at pictures again and again. They may demand to hear letters read aloud, or hear stories about the deceased. They may also carry around an object from the deceased, or hide things in special places that adults don't know about. All this keeps them close to their lost one. Such transition objects can be important as 'pain relief'. In a way the object recreates a lost reality and gives a magical support or security.

Closeness can also be sought by going to the deceased's closet and breathing in the smell that remains in the clothes, or by sleeping in Mama's or Papa's bed, taking over his or her chair, and so forth. The longing can, at least for a while, be eased through the closeness this gives. This feeling of being close to the dead one can be so strong that they have the experience that the dead one appears in their room: they see him or her in front of them, and then when they stretch out their hand to touch him or her, there is nobody there. Children that have seen their loved one following a death have sometimes voiced fear that the deceased will come back to them as they looked when they saw him or her in the casket. Preparation for these kind of experiences is important to avoid unnecessary fear and anxiety in children, but must be done with caution in order to prevent the child from waiting for such experiences with fear.

A different form of seeking to be close to the dead one occurs when the child starts to behave in ways that were characteristic of the deceased, or when they enter roles held by them. Through *identification*, or incorporation of behaviour or ways of being of the deceased, they build a kind of bridge to the deceased that eases the loss. Sometimes this gets complicated, as when children try to live up to a very clever and competent brother or sister. While some children know they are trying to be like the deceased, this happens unconsciously in others.

Sometimes children, through such identification, unconsciously console or help other family members, and sometimes they unconsciously try to be recognized and loved by being like the deceased.

Research (see Nickman, Silverman and Normand 1998; Stroebe and Schut 2006) has shown that continuing bonds to the dead person are common among children and adults alike, and associated with less grief over time. However, if they keep the relationship to the dead person too strong over time by continuously talking about the one they have lost, looking at pictures or frequenting the places they used to go with their lost one, insisting on holding on to objects they have or inherited from the one who died, it can reflect that they hold on too firmly to the relationship and may need help to go on with life.

Some children develop fantasies that they have some kind of special contact with the deceased, as if the deceased has taken up a position inside them. If the fantasies are strong or affect daily functioning it might be a sign of a complicated grief reaction, where it is best to consult mental health professionals for advice.

Usually, children will constructively seek out conversations, places and objects that help them build a bridge in their longing for the lost person, especially early after the loss, before they gradually build an inner representation of the person that they can carry throughout life. The emergence of this inner representation demands that the adults around the grieving child are willing to continue to talk with the child about the loss and the lost person. This helps them to develop and sustain an inner image of the one they have lost. This is not an easy task for a mother or father who may be grieving.

Children's different ways of seeking closeness to the dead person reflect the pain of letting what is lost go, and help them to take in the loss step by step. Parents and other adults support children in developing the inner relationship to the lost person by talking about him or her, letting children visit the grave and participate in ritual events, by letting the child have objects from the dead person (photographs, jewellery, clothes and so on), by helping them find words for feelings, by showing respect for the dead person and the child's relation to him or her, and by comforting and helping the child in easing pain and longing when necessary (Nickman *et al.* 1998). Through such activities and with an open communication climate in the family the children will fare best, and they report less depression when they reach adulthood (Saler and Skolnick 1992). It is, of course, important not to create an idyllic image of the lost person in conversations, but to have a realistic image that contains both positive, and if present, eventual negative aspects in order to confirm a child's previous experience. Children who are allowed to develop and continue such an inner relationship can allow the lost person to have a positive influence over their lifespan.

Anger and acting out

Anger and acting out is another common reaction among grieving children. Younger children often show their grief in a direct and open way. They hit and kick and say things like: 'Bad Papa that drove so fast and died.' Their anger takes different directions. It can be shown as:

- anger against death (personified) for having taken the dead person

- anger at God for letting it happen

- anger at adults because they exclude them from their grief

- anger at others for not having prevented what happened

- anger at themselves for not preventing the death

- anger at those they hold responsible for the death

- anger against the dead person because he or she has deserted them.

Children also act out in a more intense way:

A 15-year-old boy reacted with strong anger after his older brother's death. He said he wanted to throw the remote control into the TV set. He reacted with anger and frustration when faced with difficulties, for example when doing his schoolwork. At home he got out some of the tension and anger by beating his hands against the brick floor of his room. He was angry at the injustice of this world and at those he held responsible for his brother's death.

The mother of Roger (12) saw, over several years, that there was a connection between his problems both at home and at school, and his passing the anniversary of the death of his father, which happened many years before. She noticed that he became difficult, more active and more difficult to control or talk 'down' in the weeks preceding and following the anniversary for his father's death.

Temper tantrums may be apparent in the form of protest, and beating and kicking of parents. Sometimes parents are held responsible for what happened, and anger is taken out on them. Children's reactions can sometimes be a way of saving their parents from bottomless grief. Unconsciously (and consciously) they take on the task of keeping their parents from disintegrating as a consequence of the loss. Breaking windows and other unacceptable behaviour can force the parents to focus on the needs of their other children, and tear the parents loose from their depression.

Normally, boys have more difficulty than girls in putting emotions and memories into words, and in expressing grief in general. However, anger seems to be a more 'accepted' reaction in boys. We have shown how boys, compared to girls, less frequently express their grief reactions through words (Dyregrov et al. 1994). At the same time we should remember that it is well-known that sadness and depression in children often results in increased activity – where acting-out behaviour can be seen as a way of keeping sadness and depression at bay, and boys' anger may be a reflection of this.

Guilt, self-reproach and shame

Different forms of guilt, self-reproach and shame may be part of children's grief following a death. In the literature on children's grief reactions, these reactions have been given massive attention. Based on the knowledge of children's egocentric and magical thinking, it has been widely believed that children, more than adults, will think that their thoughts, feelings or actions have been the cause of what happened. Many clinical reports and case studies have emphasized the force of such reactions in children. Most of these reports have been based on children in therapy. Here parents have sought help for their children because of rather severe problems. In my own work, based on experience from follow-up of 'normal children' from all families that lost children over a three-year period in one region, problems of guilt have not been so evident (see Dyregrov 1988). By this I do not mean that children do not experience guilt reactions, but that the magnitude might have been overemphasized as a consequence of the reports being based on children in need of therapy.

Children's guilt reactions can be tied to things they have done or thought:

Five-year-old Susan had kicked her mother in her stomach during her pregnancy, and when the baby died soon after birth, Susan thought it was her fault. Her mother had, like many mothers, asked her to be careful so that nothing would happen to the baby inside her.

Marit was a young adult when I met her. All her life she had carried around guilt feelings after she as a three-year-old was away from home on the day her baby sister became so ill that she later died. 'If I had been there, it would not have happened,' she said. Guilt feelings had characterized her childhood. They had grown strong and never been met by counterarguments. It was first as an adult that she was able to deal with these feelings and thoughts.

Danny lost his mother when he was 11. When he was 16 he was sent to a psychologist because he was depressed and had dropped out of school. He strongly missed his mother and says that he almost never speaks with his father about her. During one of our sessions I ask him if there is anything he blames himself for. He looks down, ashamed, and says: 'I was so impudent with her.' When asked if he was more impudent than other boys of his age he immediately says no. He says that he has been bothered by self-reproach because he was not kind enough to his mother.

I met Sissel as an 11-year-old, four years after her mother committed suicide. On a question about whether she remember the circumstances surrounding her mother's death, she answers: 'Yes, I remember them well, and I remember that I at that time thought: "If I had tidied my room, it would not have happened."' As an 11-year-old she is able to reflect on her 'simple' way of thinking at the time, and she has dealt with the guilt feelings that no longer bother her.

When siblings die, earlier jealousy or reactions connected with differential attention during an illness may give rise to guilt. Children of preschool and early school-age will, with their egocentric and magical thought patterns, more easily think in this manner. Self-reproach can also result from how the last meeting with the dead person was, or what they never got the chance to say:

'The last thing we did was to quarrel.'
'I so much wish I could have told him how much I loved him.'
'I never got the chance to bid a proper farewell.'

It is important to note that children can think about things they did not get to do, and everything they wish that there had been time to do. Also, regarding guilt, sudden death causes a different psychological situation from anticipated death, as sudden death allows no time for goodbyes, even though it may not lead to large differences in the numbers of children who develop problems in the aftermath (Brown *et al.* 2007; Cerel *et al.* 2006).

Shame may be present with regard to how they have behaved or thought; they may experience relief at not having to share their parents' attention with a sick brother or sister any more, or they may think about what they could have done to prevent an accidental death.

If the children were present when the death happened, their guilt feelings may be more intense. This is the case with children babysitting their siblings, who either die an accidental death or die from SIDS. In these cases the self-reproach can be very hard:

> Helen (nine years old) was out strolling with her little brother (six months old) asleep in a baby carriage. When she returned to her house, her brother was dead. She blamed herself for the death, and when her parents tried to console her by saying she had no reason to blame herself, she said: 'You're only saying this to console me.' Even after receiving more information about crib death from a paediatrician, she continued to be sure that it was her fault.

Sometimes, in the heated climate that often surrounds a death, adults may say things that increase feelings of responsibility and guilt in children: 'You should have taken better care of him.'

School problems

Grief in children can lead to problems in school. First and foremost, children may experience difficulties with attention and concentration. Thoughts and memories of what has happened will interrupt their lines of thought; increased anxiety leads them to monitoring their surroundings for danger or involves thoughts about the safety of loved ones at home or at work, and sadness and grief may lead to 'slower' thinking and a lack of energy and initiative. In school they have difficulty getting their tasks done as thoughts wander, and they may memorize and learn more slowly than usual.

If they are to read aloud, they may have forgotten where to start and so forth. If they have to undertake extra tasks or burdens at home in addition, there is less time for school work. As a result their school performance may decline. The consequences of loss and trauma for school work are described in more detail elsewhere (Dyregrov 2004; Saigh *et al.* 2006).

When a death is sudden or happens in a very traumatic way, the increase in anxiety often leads to serious concentration difficulties. Being inattentive and restless can disturb the classroom. Dramatic events may also show up in the child's work, where traumatic elements appear in drawings, compositions and other activities the child engages in.

School problems are especially common following the death of parents, and have only received educational interest in later years. While many other problems disappear during the first year, school performance following the loss of a loved one can continue throughout the first years following the loss.

Physical complaints

Bodily complaints, in the form of an increase in headaches, stomach complaints or sore muscles, are all known to appear in some grieving children. Such complaints get a lot of adult attention, and this may reinforce the symptoms by the secondary gains the children get from this. In families where children have died, similar complaints to those the deceased showed appearing in a sibling can trigger alarm reactions in the parents. When complaints parallel those of the deceased, a family's anxiety that the same thing will happen all over again gets intense. Sometimes the children themselves directly relate their bodily reactions to the death:

> Less than three weeks following her father's accidental death, three-year-old Cecilia's mother calls me up late one night and is upset because her daughter has high fever and vomits. It was not the fact that she was sick that triggered her call, but a question and comment Cecilia had made: 'Mama, do you know why I am sick?' Her mother had answered that she did not, to which the little girl said: 'It is because I am so sad that my daddy is dead.' When a three-year-old can express such an understanding of the relation of body and mind, no wonder her mother was upset.

Other possible grief reactions

It is difficult to separate the usual grief reactions from those less frequent. I have chosen to use the expression 'possible grief reactions' to suggest that the reactions now being described are a bit less common than those already described. The separation is somewhat haphazard, but is based on many conversations with parents and children.

Among the possible grief reactions are:

- regressive behaviour
- social isolation
- fantasies
- personality changes
- pessimism about the future
- preoccupation with cause and meaning
- maturing and growing.

Regressive behaviour

Children at all ages can show different forms of regressive behaviour. Smaller children may start wetting their bed, become more clinging and so forth. Older children seek the closeness of adults and may become clinging in their own way, and behave more childishly for a period, maybe by using 'babyish' language or tone. This can be very demanding of parents or the remaining parent, as they lack the energy to handle such reactions.

Social isolation

Some children will isolate themselves from peers and others following a loss. This social isolation can be caused by a lack of understanding among their peers:

> A 12-year-old found that his schoolmates mocked him because his father was dead, and because he didn't have a father. He was bullied and felt stigmatized, as if everybody could see that his father had died of cancer.

Teenagers may be wary of the conceptions or beliefs connected with different diseases, especially cancerous diseases. Such diseases have many negative connotations for both children and adults. When in grief we are more vulnerable to others' comments, and they easily trigger hurtful feelings. Some children worry about the questions that schoolmates might ask about the death, because they are afraid of crying at school. They fear the embarrassment they may feel if they lose control of their feelings. Children may guard against this by pulling away from their surroundings. Often children do not know how to deal with the new situation that arises when a friend experiences a death in his or her family, and they may solve the difficult situation by avoiding contact. In addition, such deaths may challenge friends' sense of security, and give rise to thoughts that this might happen to someone close to them.

In some families children are sent away to stay with friends or family when a death occurs. Sometimes the family even moves away. This leads to a breakdown of the child's network. For adolescents the problems are reinforced by the fact that many change their life priorities and feel that their peers are interested in unimportant things. They can value their loved ones more than before, their experience makes them more sure of themselves, they can become better at talking about difficult things, and they know how to care for others who go through a difficult time. Many say that they are better able to discriminate between what is important and what is unimportant. This accelerated maturity may lead them to feel more mature than their friends, and to perceive their friends as immature. In turn they may withdraw from their peers and friends and seek contact with those that are older than themselves. Taken together, such factors can account for the fact that some children become more socially isolated following a death in the family. When they seek out older adolescents this can accelerate their development even more, in a way that means they take on habits and ways of being inappropriate for their age, with the frustration this can cause in caretakers.

Fantasies

Children may make up various fantasies about the death or the dead person. These often originate in misperceptions based on limited information given by adults. These fantasies can easily become frightening. They may be fantasies about the cause of death, fantasies about the dead person coming back to revenge him or herself, or fantasies about what the dead person looks like. Bits of information that the child picks up are put together with what they already know, and are assimilated into the fantasies and concepts they already have about death. Because they also may have vivid experiences of the dead person being close to them, this can lead to an intensification of fear and new fantasies.

Personality changes

A child may change character after someone close dies. Such personality changes do not need to be dramatic, but may appear in the form of the child becoming more quiet and isolated, or more anxious and afraid. Traumatic deaths, especially the death of a parent, will increase the chance of a more permanent personality change, often exacerbated by the lack of adequate help to deal with the trauma.

Pessimism about the future

Years ago Leonore Terr (1979, 1983) showed how children who experienced extreme stress lost their faith in their own future. They may have difficulty envisioning growing up, getting married and having children. Although such loss of a future perspective may not be common among children who lose a loved one, research does show that young adults who have lost parents during their childhood expect to have a shorter lifespan than others of the same age (Denes-Raj and Ehrlichman 1991). Such reactions may appear if the death happened under especially traumatic circumstances, such as when violence is involved. The gnawing uncertainty or vulnerability that many children experience can be a signal that pessimism is only a step away. Pessimism about the future seems to be related to traumatic anxiety, where the fear of something new happening cast shadows into the future.

Preoccupation with thoughts about cause and meaning

Preoccupation with thoughts about cause and meaning often enters children's thoughts. Why did it happen? Why did it happen to us? How did it happen? The injustice, God's meaning and the search for explanations may preoccupy the child, both in the short and long term:

> Cecilia (three years old) played with a friend and was very preoccupied with why her father died (he died in an accident). Her way of expressing her feeling that the normal sequence of life was turned upside down was: 'I think it is so strange that Papa could die before Grandma.' Three years of age, and still occupied by the same thoughts that adults find so hard to reconcile themselves with.

Maturity and growing

Children may also show growth and increased maturity following a death in the family. They may increase their ability to show compassion and consideration for others (become less self-centred), they may understand their parents better, and they may be proud of being of help.

The difference between trauma and grief

It is important to differentiate between after-effects, caused by the traumatic nature of a death, and grief reactions. Sudden deaths will often be dramatic for adults and children alike. The shock when the death becomes known is totally different from a death where there has been time for preparation. When a death occurs suddenly, the child's reactions are partly caused by the nature of the death and the way they are told about it, and partly by the loss itself. Maybe we understand this difference better if we think about a situation where the child witnesses a death, or finds the dead body of a parent who has committed suicide. In such situations the event will 'burn' itself into the brain in a way other than with anticipated deaths, and the child's security is gravely undermined in a brutal way.

PTSD may develop where children witness a death or harbour fantasies about how a loved one died. This complicates children's grief reactions as this disorder contains reactions involving intrusive recollections (or fantasies) from what they experienced, trying to avoid such material and a body that becomes hyper-aroused. If a child, as part of usual grief, is approaching thoughts or memories about their loved one, the intrusive material can emerge and produce intense distress. It can be difficult thinking of good memories because every time the child does so, it activates the memories about how the loved one died. This makes it very important to prioritize the reduction of the post-traumatic reactions. Worden (1996) described the following tasks for children in grief:

- accepting the reality of the loss
- experiencing the pain or emotional aspects of the loss
- adjusting to an environment in which the deceased is missing
- relocating the dead person within one's life and finding ways to memorialize the person.

As trying to cope with post-traumatic reactions easily leads to avoidant behaviour as well as avoidance and suppression of thoughts, the tasks described are complicated if the child suffers from PTSD.

Unfortunately, my experience, as that of others (Cohen *et al.* 2002), is that the children that do not get help in working through the traumatic aspects of a death experience more problems in their grief work. To prevent unnecessary after-effects from the death, adults must be provided with a greater understanding of children's need to work through the trauma as well as the grief. The problems many children suffer in their grief originates in anxiety related to the circumstances of the death.

My experience, and that of others (Kaplow *et al.* 2006), is that children who do not work through the traumatic circumstances of a death may slow down or stop in their grieving process. After sudden, dramatic deaths, adults must help children work through their impressions about what happened, or contact mental health professionals who can help in this process. Children with PTSD can also experience extreme fear of a new death and this fear makes it difficult to relate to the loss. Cohen and co-workers (2002) have outlined the differences between normal and complicated bereavement in more detail.

Chapter Two

Different types
of death

———◆———

The death of a parent

Among different types of deaths, the death of a parent has the greatest consequences for a child. Not only do they lose a person who is responsible for love and daily care, but the death often leads to less stability and an overturning of their daily life. Most children will deny aspects of the finality of their parent's death. Such a death is so penetrating that the child needs to keep the realities at a distance, not so that they lose contact with reality, but because the emotional magnitude can only be taken in step by step.

Signs of this immediate, automatic emotional defence or protection mechanism may often be seen immediately after they get the message – many do not cry, some start to laugh, and many immediately start being very direct and practical, which is shown in questions or comments such as:

'Can I use his bed now?'
'Can I have his grey jacket?'
'Can I take part in the funeral?'
'I am the man in the family now.'

There is a strong need to keep what has happened at a distance, and to let the event get closer gradually. Owing to their lack of tolerance for strong reactions, thoughts about the event can be pushed out of conscious awareness for longer periods of time, and the child may behave as he or she normally does. Strong feelings may appear in other situations (displaced feelings), such as when they watch a film, read a book or hear about others who suffer for some reason. Then their emotional expression can be stronger than the situation might appear to warrant. In this way they may show their reactions, isolated from the death.

As a bridge to the lost one, they may develop fantasies that he or she will come back. Children may also replay what happened internally or through play and let everything end happily, as if nothing has happened. Fantasies of reunion are common, and children may express the wish to die them-selves so that they may be reunited with their loved one:

> Nigel was only five, but clearly expressed that he wanted to die to join his daddy up in heaven. Naturally his mother became very concerned when he also stated how he would do this: by strangling himself with a rope.

The last contact with the dead person is of considerable importance for many children. Sometimes things that happened just before the death are given a supernatural expla-nation, as an omen or warning of what was about to happen, or things are given a special meaning, for example as showing them how to make choices for the future. Through anger and fury against their surroundings children may also try to force their parent back to life.

Although the majority of children who lose close family members will cope well in childhood and adult life, the loss of a parent is statistically associated with an increase in vulnera-bility for psychological problems, especially depression, in both child- and adulthood (Dowdney 2000; Kaufman and Kaufman 2006; Mack 2001; Pfeffer *et al.* 2007; Siegel, Karus and Raveis 1996). It is evident that it is not only the loss that leads to an increase in problems for the child, but also the consequences that the loss has for the family in the form of more pressure on the remaining parent, economic difficulties and other negative life events or factors in its wake. It is especially an increase in depression and suicides that has been reported. This risk is increased if:

- the death was sudden

- it happened to an 'older' child

- the child lacks an adequate replacement figure (Parker and Manicavasagar 1986).

While earlier reports showed that more than one-third of children who lost parents struggled with depression a year following their loss (Black and Urbanowicz 1987; Weller *et al.* 1991), newer and methodologically more sound studies in the field conclude that around 20% of all children who lose a parent display an array of emotional and behavioural symptoms in the aftermath, such as anxiety and depression, anger outbursts and loss of functions they already mastered (regression) (Cerel *et al.* 2006). Reactions may come a long time following the loss, and in an important study by Worden and Silverman (1996) 21% of children who lost a parent still had serious problems two years after the loss.

Reinherz and co-workers (1999) followed children through their childhood into adult life to look at risk factors for the development of depression. They found that following their parent's death girls were more at risk for depression than boys, but only if it was their mother that died. Other studies have also documented that girls are more at risk following parental loss (Raveis, Siegel and Karus 1999; Silverman and Worden 1992). Loss of a mother seems especially difficult for children (Saler and Skolnick 1992;

Silverman and Worden 1992). This probably reflects mothers still taking care of more important caring functions than fathers, and maybe also the fact that fathers struggle to establish a warm, open caring climate in the home following the loss. Most men have less experience from childhood in using language and conversations in the wake of emotionally upsetting events, a fact that seems to be especially hard if mothers die and fathers are to sustain the emotional climate at home. It may also reflect that girls either take on or have to take on more tasks in the home if the mother dies, in relation to siblings and the father, and that this care pressure results in long-term negative consequences.

Another issue that might complicate the situation for girls is the early remarriage of fathers after their wife's death. Campbell and Silverman (1996) write that among American widowers 52% have remarried within 18 months following the loss of their partner. Riches and Dawson (2000) have in detail described the problem this causes for girls. They postulate that fathers in general are less sensitive to emotions and provide less depth in interpersonal relations, and that this is especially hard on teenage girls, as their grief follows a different course from their fathers. Regardless of the reasons for the girls' vulnerability, the knowledge we have indicates that girls should be monitored closely following their mother's death.

Adam *et al.* (1982) have shown that more than half of a group of students who had lost a parent before the age of 16 had serious suicidal thoughts, compared to 10% in a control group. Weller and co-workers (1991) found that 61% of children who had lost a parent had suicidal thoughts, but no one had tried to commit suicide. With the knowledge we have that parents (Stoppelbein and Greening 2000), and especially fathers (Weller *et al.* 1991), often underestimate how children experience the situation; it is important to have a good follow-up of both children and parents. This shows how important it is to secure adequate help for remaining parents and carers following such deaths, to make sure that children's needs are taken care of properly.

During the first years of life, a child is dependent on the parents to have their physical and psychological needs met. When small children lose a parent, they lose a person who satisfies such primary needs, and they react to this. When small children lose a parent, the remaining parent also loses a partner – with the consequences this can have. This can lead to a temporary or permanent reduction in parental capacity. This is, of course, nothing that the parent can be blamed for, but it may follow that the fine-tuned interplay between child and parent can be disturbed. Later research has shown that depression in parents, especially mothers, has a clear negative influence on parental caring capacity, and although grieving parents have not been the focus of much research, there is some research that indicates that the capacity to parent is also influenced by grief (Cerel *et al.* 2006). Depression in mothers especially seems to affect emotional regulation among girls (Silk *et al.* 2006). Such findings make it very important to offer adequate counselling and help to parents of preschool children. Tiffany Field and co-workers (Feijo *et al.* 2006; Field *et al.* 1996) have shown that relatively simple advice to parents about physical closeness and contact with their children, including simple body massage, can counteract such negative effects. When mothers massage their children it reduces anxiety and depression in mothers as well (Feijo *et al.* 2006).

It is not only depression in parents that can make a grieving child's situation problematic. If the death has resulted in post-traumatic problems for parents or the remaining parent, children will evidence more problems (Stoppelbein and Greening 2000). There are several explanations for this, many paralleling those mentioned for depression, but the important implications are that parents receive adequate help with their own problems in order for them to be there for their grieving children.

Even for older children the remaining parent's ability to establish positive parenting is important for the child's adaptation to the loss (Haine *et al.* 2006). By this is meant that the remaining parent is able to sustain discipline at the same time as they manage to have a home characterized by warmth, care and respect. Children's emotional needs must be taken care of while they are stimulated to meet the demands and challenges that follow the age they are moving through. It is difficult for parents in grief to ensure that conflict and problem-solving takes place in a positive climate when one is alone with the caring tasks, and grief in itself may drain one of energy. When remaining parents meet in groups that directly stimulate such positive parenting, it leads to good results for children who lose a parent (Tein, Sandler and Ayers 2006).

Idealizing the dead person poses a special problem for some children, as it precludes the open expression of anger against them. If only the positive sides can be talked about, the child's anger toward his or her parent for deserting him or her cannot be expressed. This anger may then be directed toward the child's surroundings. Such reactions make it difficult for the remaining parent when he or she wants to enter into a new relationship, or for 'replacement' parents who are taking care of children when both parents are dead. Such problems also arise when children demand that family routines, attitudes and rules remain as they were before:

> Linda (16) was furious when her mother was going to a cinema with a male friend a little more than a year following her father's death. When I asked her how long time following the death it would be appropriate to allow passing before her mother could date another man, she hissed: 'Never'.

After the death of a parent, some pre-adolescents and adolescents can prematurely be 'forced' into an adult role, where they have to take on responsibilities that are not appropriate to their age. Many adolescents have functioned as surrogate mothers or fathers for their younger siblings. This is not solely negative – on the contrary, it can stimulate growth and maturity if it happens without the 'replacement role' taking predominance. A role as supporter or replacement mother or father that is too onerous may result in inadequate work as a result of the child's own grief and the loss of important aspects of their own childhood. A mutually supportive relationship, where the remaining parent and children help each other, is to be highly valued, however, as it emphasizes the child's feeling of maturity, independence and progress toward the adult role. Even small children can sometimes understand and express their experience of the role changes that take place in the family:

> A boy of six who lost his craftsman father said right after his death: 'He does not need his tools any more. I am the man in the house now.' The same boy checked his mother's reactions by stating 'Raise a hand if you think it is sad.'

If a parent's death is caused by violence, anxiety and fear may be very deep, often increased by the talk among peers. If the death is caused by other family members, both fantasies and fear are increased: 'Everybody says they never believed that he could do a thing like that. Could my father do something similar?', 'What makes somebody do something like that?'

After a violent death, smaller children often let their play circle around the trauma:

> A small girl who witnessed her baby brother being killed by a family member played out what happened repeatedly. She also made a prison in her play where she made sure that the murderer was kept.

Bergen (1958) mentions a four-year-old who witnessed the murder of one of her parents and who painted her hands red and played a game where she stabbed herself with a paint brush. Older children may immediately plan how they will protect their remaining parent against threats.

In our work with war situations we often see how smaller children can draw or repeat in play or behaviour what they witnessed or heard about. If one of their parents has been killed they immediately start planning how they shall protect the remaining parent against threats.

Luckily, following violent deaths, many children identify with the helpers or the good-doers. They may express wishes of becoming a nurse or a doctor when they grow up, or they want to become a police officer. It is evident that this reflects their need to control future events, that they want to reverse their helplessness and be able to enter into roles that control 'life and death'. Some have their future occupations made out for themselves.

Grief, longing and pain following the death of parents and other loved ones may be particularly strong or return at anniversary dates, such as the birthday of the dead person or the day he or she died, as well as at Christmas, New Year or Easter. A ritual marking is very helpful in relation to such anniversaries. This helps the child to give concrete expression of their feelings surrounding such days.

It should be clearly pointed out that a child who loses a parent is not doomed to a life of problems. Although statistics show that children who lose a parent develop more problems than those who don't, most children fare well or as well as children without parental loss (Pfeffer *et al.* 2000). Children's ability to cope with the loss will, not least, be associated with how the remaining parent is able to create a climate in the family where the child can talk about their lost parent over time if they wish to, have their emotional needs cared for and experience understanding in kindergarten or school and among friends.

The death of a sibling

Children's reactions after a sibling's death will be similar to those following a parent's death, but the intensity, duration and long-term consequences are usually less.

Research has shown mixed results concerning the consequences of sibling loss, from very extensive and strong reactions to relatively mild reactions (see Brent *et al.* 1996; Hogan and Greenfield, 1991). We have written more extensively about siblings' reactions elsewhere (Dyregrov and Dyregrov 2005), and will briefly describe here some important aspects of such deaths.

When a child dies it will have an impact on the emotional climate in the home. Remaining siblings not only experience the loss of a playmate and rival, but for a period lose parental attention and care as well. They witness strong reactions in their parents, and they become the centre of their parents' fear that something will happen to them as well. The parents' lack of energy and their intense grief makes it more difficult for them to set limits than before. Parents may also experience a bad conscience because they do not spend enough time with their other children, and guilt always reduces boundaries. This can have unfortunate consequences, especially during adolescence. Long and hard work might be needed to 'take up the reins' again. Counselling about such consequences can help to prevent or reduce such problems.

The loss of a sibling may also affect later-born children as well. Parents' anxiety can result in overprotection that hinders the child's development of independence, or the new child can be forced to 'fill the footsteps' of the lost child. This can impede the formation of their own identity. British researchers have shown that following stillbirth there is a clear increase in attachment problems in later-born children, reflecting that the mother's anxiety for the child influences the development of the child in a negative way and that they end up having more problems than children without such a loss of a sibling (Hughes *et al.* 2001).

The child's order and position in the family may influence his or her reaction. If younger siblings die, guilt feelings can be strong because of wishes to get rid of the child, while children who lose older siblings may be strained by the burden of filling the footsteps of, and having to replace, the dead child and being the focus of their parents' attention.

After the death of a child there is potential for over-protection, scapegoating and pressure on siblings to take over the dead child's role and personality. On the positive side, as time goes by, parents realize what they stand to lose and become more caring of their remaining children. Many children will, together with their parents, work through the loss and come through what happened as a strengthened family. The death of a child often means a re-allocation of roles among the remaining siblings, in addition to the emotional vacuum the dead child leaves behind.

A child's death causes a great strain on the family system, and a different tempo in the two partners' processing of their grief may lead to profound conflict between them. Even though research has not provided an unequivocal answer to the question of whether a child's death results in an increased divorce rate, it is a fact that it results in an increased strain on the relationship (Dyregrov 1990). Remaining children live in this field of tension and are not, of course, unaffected by it.

It has been pointed out earlier that deaths where children are present when their sibling dies, for example as babysitters at a sudden infant death syndrome (SIDS) death or playing when an accidental death occurs, can cause more severe problems. Not only may children blame themselves for what happened, but adults may more or less consciously lay the burden of what happened on the child. If this happens in a moment of strong distress, it can be damaging, but the damage can be reduced by talking openly and frankly with the child about what happened. It is more damaging if such 'explosive outbursts' are never mentioned again, when parents, in their fear of their own anger at their child's involvement, do not mention their outburst with so much as a single word, or if they repeat the accusations. This increases the likelihood of difficulty in the child's grief reaction.

Self-reproach and guilt are also found in siblings, as sibling relationships often include ambivalent feelings. Strong jealousy, or a negative relationship between siblings, can increase grief-related problems. If the death resulted from an illness, it is not uncommon for siblings to be the target for the sick child's anger over his or her own situation and future, with mutual anger as a result. Sometimes well children can even wish that their sick brother or sister was dead. When death occurs, guilt, self-reproach and shame may increase their grief. When there is a sudden death, an angry or negative last meeting may also result in such reactions.

So-called 'survivor guilt' can sometimes be seen among siblings: 'It should not have been him who died, but me. He was so clever at everything.' Sometimes this is an appeal to parents to state that they are worth as much as the child who died. The long-term consequences for the child's emotional development will depend on age, maturity level and the way the event is handled by adults.

Frederick was 13 when his older brother died in a tragic event. He reacted with shock and feelings of unreality. Two years later he felt depressed, partly because he blamed himself for not reacting enough, partly because he thought that his parents loved his successful, good at school brother more than him, who did not excel at school. He needed to have repeated some information he received close in time to the death about how a shock reaction often keeps emotions at bay, and in addition it was good for him to have his memory jolted on how he had hit his knuckles on a concrete floor in desperation and anger over what had happened to his brother. He was also reassured about his parents' love and that their preoccupation with their loss did not reflect less love for him.

When a child dies, this will most often be a much greater and more enduring strain on the parents than on the remaining siblings. When children only show their grief in short periods of time, or they refrain from showing their grief to their parents, it is not surprising that parents sometimes accuse their remaining children of not grieving sufficiently. Fortunately, it is not common for parents to say this directly to their children; but it is a fact that many parents are concerned about siblings' 'lack of grief'. It is important that parents do not place unrealistic and unreasonable demands on the magnitude and type of grief the child should show. What might be seen as strange and unsuitable for adults in an early grief period is often not similarly inappropriate for children:

> A girl who learnt about her sister's death on the same day that she was to attend a carnival, insisted on going. Her grandfather became furious over this, and said that it was quite improper. The girl cried and finally got permission to go. Her grandfather and other family members needed orientation about children's grief reactions to understand her reaction.

When schoolchildren die, siblings are often exposed to many questions from the dead child's peers. They may feel as if they are being pumped for information, both while their sister or brother is ill, and after the death. This is sometimes so hard to tolerate that they want to stay away from school:

> A boy whose only brother was dying experienced going to school as a nightmare. He was stopped daily on his way to school and asked for information on how his brother fared. Finally his father had to drive him to school, as he could not stand this any more.

When a child dies, it challenges children's as well as adults' assumptions about the world. When a child dies, they die at the wrong end of life, and this is something that interferes with other children's sense of security in the world ('This can happen to me too'), the meaning of existence and their sense of justice. A child's death is experienced as deeply unjust – it is the elderly and sick that should die, not those with life in front of them.

Siblings' worries about getting the same illness or being killed themselves are not uncommon, adding to their increased fear and anxiety. Not only do parents become very concerned when the sibling feels sick, but siblings themselves may worry that they will also die.

Against this background, it is understandable that a child's death requires siblings to develop new assumptions about the world, to comprehend that accepted truths do not hold and that the secure basis of their existence must be founded on new ground. Both regarding thoughts and feelings, this means an adaption or change, in which adults' ability to listen, take part in and support the child's development of a changed basis for their existence is fundamental.

The death of a grandparent
Children often form strong bonds with their grandparents, and the death of a grandparent can make a great impression on them. They may react with grief and long to see them

again. However, this grief is of another character than when a parent or sibling dies.

When a death happens in the grandparents' generation, it happens to an elderly person, and this is easier for the child to understand, as it is in harmony with the concepts they have formed, and their knowledge of death as the end of a long life. A grandparent's death does not challenge their assumptions about death and the world as dramatically as the death of a younger person, and thus it is somewhat easier to understand such deaths both emotionally and intellectually.

Usually a child does not lose his or her firm basis of existence when a grandparent dies. Their daily needs are taken care of by parents. But they may feel that they are 'sent away' to others, or that they are shut out from the adult world. This may lead to fear of separation and may foster anxiety. At the same time a grandparent's death may result in anxiety that other loved ones will also die.

Children's reactions may be much stronger if they have daily contact with their grandparents, for example when they live with them, or when the grandparents cared for them while their parents were at work.

The death of a friend

Throughout childhood, friends become increasingly important for children. In adolescence, friends are, in certain domains, more important than parents. Friendly relationships can be intense, and many friendships are formed that last throughout life. Strong peer relationships knit adolescents together, often with dramatic break-ups and reunions.

We have little knowledge about what a death means when a dear friend or girlfriend or boyfriend dies. Little research has been conducted, and this situation is not often mentioned in clinical reports. My experience is that the adult world has greatly overlooked the effect that the death of a friend has on close friends and classmates.

All the reactions mentioned earlier can be seen after a friend's death. But such grief reactions are often not recognized by adults, and children do not get much chance to talk about what has happened. During school days the focus is often on the class (or group) that the child belonged to and best friends may not be recognized if they are outside this class (group) (Dyregrov *et al.* 1999a). When adults refrain from talking with children about such events, it can be seen partly as reluctance on the part of the parents to acknowledge that children die, as this involves admitting that the same can happen to their own children. But this is exactly what the child might need to talk about. In a study dating back to 1999 we showed that the death of a classmate led to strong reactions among around one-fifth of the remaining class students as long as nine months following the death (Dyregrov, Bie Wikander and Vigerust 1999b). These effects were, of course, not limited to the class, but also included close friends outside the class.

Unfortunately, it seems that the death of a friend is not talked about for long among peers either. That John was Eugene's best friend is soon forgotten. Older children, especially boys, may have difficulty showing their grief. Therefore the grief can be very lonely. Embittered feelings triggered by the injustice of one's friend's death, or survival guilt where the child either wants to exchange place with the dead person or be reunited with him or her, can be strong feelings following a death in adolescence. Following a discothèque fire in Göteborg in 1999 we undertook a study of adolescents from different schools throughout the city and showed that the closer they felt to those who died the stronger were their reactions in the aftermath (Dyregrov *et al.* 2003).

Older children identify with their friends and develop fantasies about how this would have been for them. What would my last thoughts have been just before I died? How did he feel then? Did it hurt?

When a friend dies suddenly, for example when playing on the ice or while participating in some 'forbidden' activity, the question about death as the punishment for illegal behaviour will be important for the child to talk about. Parents, maybe to conquer their fear that this might happen to their children, sometimes use what has happened to frighten children from participating in dangerous activities. When death is portrayed as the punishment for having been bad or as the result of having taken part in prohibited activities, this can be an extra burden for children. It is an adult's task to help children separate these issues and prevent misunderstandings.

Adolescents might lose a boy- or girlfriend who has been important for sexual exploration and maturity. Such relationships are seldom sanctioned by the adult world, and it may be embedded in guilt feelings. It can be difficult to talk to someone about intense longings, or about thoughts that the death was a punishment for doing 'bad' things. As adults we need to acknowledge and understand more of what it means to lose friends or steady dates. Few places is this clearer than on the internet where commemoration of dead friends has spread throughout many Western countries.

Children and suicide

Suicide creates a difficult situation for both bereaved adults and children. For the child such deaths challenge their thoughts about what people can do, and touch upon their own destructive impulses, their helplessness and dependence. Children may believe that the dead person did not love them, that they themselves failed, and they feel deeply deserted and let down. Older children may ruminate on the tendency to commit suicide as hereditary, and fear that they will do the same. Children who experience that their parent commited suicide struggle more than children who lose a parent to other causes (Cerel *et al.* 1999). This may not only reflect the mode of death, but also the home climate preceding the death. In our work we have documented the very difficult situation that siblings experience following a sibling or parent's death (Dyregrov and Dyregrov 2005).

Children may accidentally be part of what happened, as when parents have made plans that the children should be somewhere else when the act takes place. Children may also be witness to, or find, the dead body. Sometimes they are made more actively part of the preparations for the suicide, as when they have picked up the pills or bought the razor blades that were used to commit the act. Sometimes they know about aspects that may explain why a sibling took his or her own life, but because they promised never to tell, or they do not want to add to the pain their parents experience, they carry this knowledge around without being able to express it. Such factors will increase and complicate the working through of grief. We have written more about children and families' situations elsewhere (Dyregrov and Dyregrov 2004, 2005).

Smaller children, but sometimes adolescents as well, may recreate what happened in play and in their behaviour. Adults may become very frightened if the child asks what will happen if they take six or eight pills, or in some other way indicate that they harbour thoughts about suicide. Such things do not necessarily mean that the child actively plans to take his or her life; the child may only be trying to get a grip on what has happened. It adds fear when a nine-year-old asks if classmates will come to his funeral if he dies, and such questions should lead to a talk with the child about the thoughts and fantasies he or she has, to give them an opportunity to talk about their inner turmoil – and necessary precautions should be taken if the child really harbours suicidal thoughts and plans. If a child, in addition to talking, changes usual habits or behaviour such as eating habits, withdrawing from their social environment or friends, or wants to give away important and dear possessions, adults should quickly secure the help of professionals:

> A seven-year-old boy was preoccupied by the question of whether his father committed suicide because he was angry at him. He was also very sad that his father wrote a letter to his mother and not to him. His continuous preoccupation with his parent's death prompted his mother to contact a health professional.

Children may attach special meaning to certain details present in relation to the death, such as the fact that they bought the instrument that was used; they may be bothered by intense recollections, or they may in their behaviour or in fantasy take part in rituals that they believe can prevent a repetition of the event.

Most suicides happen through violent means, such as jumping from a building, hanging, shooting, crashing a car and so forth. Unfortunately, adults have an even stronger tendency to shut children off from information about what happened following suicide than after other deaths. All our experience indicates that children know and understand more than they admit to adults. Often, this knowledge is something they actively acquire through talking to friends who have overheard their parents talking, by hearing something in a shop and so forth. It is important that the child is promptly informed to prevent the spreading of lack of trust of the adult world: 'When they could keep me from knowing this fact for weeks, what else may they hide from me?'

Inadequate or incorrect explanations increase the chances for self-reproach, as they prevent children from discussing their thoughts and fantasies. It is important to listen for indications that the child blames him or herself, for example by asking: 'What do you think made your mother take so many pills?'

> A 17-year-old sibling after suicide was full of self-reproach because she had not understood what was in the making: 'I should have understood it from our last telephone conversation. I am the eldest sibling and should have understood.'

When parents do not tell children the truth, and, for example 'rewrite' it by stating that the heart failed, they have to live with an ever-present nagging fear that the truth might surface through somebody's careless comment, or accidentally through the child's friends. If the truth is revealed in this or other ways, the trust between parents and children can be forever weakened. A white lie that is used at the start to spare the child can therefore lead to great problems for both adults and children in the long run. Children are also much less prepared to deal with friends' questions or information if they are uninformed about the background of the death. When children are openly told about the suicide, and they are given the opportunity to discuss with adults how to answer friends' questions, as well as to receive help in how to handle different situations outside home, they are better able to deal with the situation.

It is known that, following suicide, parents may press children to shut away or deny things they have observed, things that adults do not want them to have experienced. They may be told that what they saw was not really what they saw, that a suicide was an accident or that the death was caused by an illness. They might even be ridiculed or told they were confused or had a dream. When this happens, the child may develop more serious psychiatric problems, often with distrust of others, lack of trust of their own senses, feelings of unreality and so forth.

Suicide attempts can also be hard for children to face. Such attempts will alter the parent–child relationship. The suicide attempter often feels even more helpless following the attempt, and can be left with a sense of incompetence concerning his or her responsibility for his or her children. The children, on their side, may feel intense fear of a repetition, or they may feel responsible for the suicide attempt. They may take on responsibility for their father or mother, and start changing their everyday behaviour to make sure they can hinder repetition through proper planning: 'If I hide her pills somewhere in the garden, do you think she would find them then?' They may also demand promises or guarantees from their parent that they will not repeat the attempt, parallel to the contracts that therapists make with their patients in similar situations. Sometimes they explain away or take on responsibility for what happened, and in that way create some kind of 'inner peace'.

We still know relatively little about cluster suicides. Even though several suicides among children or adolescents may happen in a relatively short period of time in the same area, it is not well known in what way grief may have been a contributing factor, or whether one suicide may have acted as a 'model' for others. Because adolescents are in the process of forming their identity and experiencing inner and outer changes in their lives, and because the peer group has become a dominant influence on their behaviour, the possibility of romanticizing death through suicide is possible. News about an adolescent suicide in school may therefore be seen as a romantic escape from an otherwise difficult situation. Together with what seems to be a decreased tolerance for pain, this may contribute to the increase in children and adolescent suicides that has been evident during recent years. There is some empirical evidence indicating that adolescents who have survived the suicide of a loved one are at greater risk of suicide themselves. The failure to grieve seems to increase this risk further (see Valente, Saunders and Street 1988). The fact that there is a risk of cluster suicide makes it important how such events are handled in the school and the local community. In the school it is possible to assess (screen) classmates and best friends for suicidal risk. There are some data indicating that good crisis intervention, where what happened is dealt with in a concrete, non-romanticizing way, can reduce the risk of new suicides (Poijula, Wahlberg and Dyregrov 2001a). Among important signs to look out for regarding the risk of suicide in children are:

- preoccupation with themes of death or expressing suicidal thoughts
- giving away prized possessions
- appearance of peace, relief, contentment, especially following a period of unrest; this signals that a decision is made and often follows the second sign above
- sudden and extreme changes in eating habits
- withdrawal from friends and family or other major behavioural changes or the opposite, in the form of aggression
- changes in sleeping patterns
- changes in school performance.

(From *The Crisis Management Manual (Revised)*, developed by the Afton Oaks Hospital, San Antonio, 1989.)

The Norwegian psychologist Magne Raundalen has provided a very useful 'recipe' on how parents (or remaining parent) can tell and explain in a simple and direct way why some people take their own life. This explanation can be used for quite small children. If it is a parent that commits suicide he explains it as an illness in the thoughts called 'depression' (not applicable in all situations). He then draws the thoughts as green and fresh long vertical lines, sometimes with flowers on. For thoughts to remain fresh and green the brain needs light and warmth. When one gets the disease named depression, it becomes dark and cold where the thoughts are, and they start to wither. If it becomes very cold and dark inside, the thought that one can go and get help also withers. Brown and black colours are used to illustrate the withering thoughts as leaves in autumn. The last thoughts that wither are the thoughts about one's children, illustrated as green lines among the brown and dark ones. If these thoughts also grow ill, the person thinks: I cannot even take care of myself, how can I then be a father/mother to my children? Raundalen also describes concretely how the mode of death can be explained to children:

> Then there is only one thought left and it is ill. It is a dark thought inside the brain and it says: I must die. I must travel to death. That is the only place for me now. And to die one has to stop breathing and to stop breathing one has to put a rope around one's throat and that is called hanging. Or to end breathing I have to fill my lungs with water. That is called drowning. Or to die I have to tap out all my blood. That can be done by cutting one's pulse or putting a knife into one's heart. To die one has to stop the heart from beating and that can be done by very strong medicine. Or to die one has to take away all thoughts. That can be done by shooting a bullet into the brain. (Raundalen 2000 – translation by the author).

Depending on the way the suicide was committed an explanation is chosen.

Other deaths

Other deaths may also have a great effect on children. This is certainly so when good friends lose their parents. Such deaths make them vulnerable to thoughts about the same thing happening to their own loved ones. Their more or less developed illusion of invulnerability ('this will not happen here or to me and my loved one') are replaced by feelings of insecurity and the understanding that this can also happen to them.

When a parent dies, this leads to a lot of questions in friends' homes: 'Who will take care of Carol now?', 'Why do adults drive so fast?', 'Will you promise to be careful?', 'Does Greg have to move?'

Some children may show separation anxiety; they do not want to go to the play group and they become more clinging, having a greater need to be in their parents' close and safe presence. Most of all, they need parents to talk openly with them about what happened. It is a misconception on the part of adults if they refrain from talking about what has happened so as not to frighten the child with their own reactions. Silence and suppression is almost always a source of anxiety for children.

The death of well-known public figures, such as Diana, Princess of Wales, and other disastrous events such as the September 11, 2001 terrorist attack on the World Trade Center and various school shootings also have an effect on children. The effect of such media-mediated effects on children is described by Otto and co-workers (2007) and Saylor and co-workers (2003).

Chapter Three

Death and crisis at different developmental levels

Preschool children

Preschool children face many important developmental tasks. They are learning to trust others; they are developing their basic security and forming basic attachments to others. Gradually they develop control over their body and impulses, develop their identity and autonomy, and seek to understand their outer world.

In death or crisis situations, they are at the most helpless and passive age. They are most dependent on help from adults to regain balance. At the same time they may have a reduced capacity for understanding what is happening, and they do not have the capacity, as older children have, to change what has happened in fantasy to regain control and reduce anxiety. Children at this age often have a heightened sense of anxiety concerning separations and rejections, and are thus more vulnerable when the death of a primary carer occurs. They may often ask for the dead person, and there may be intense searching for the lost one. Sometimes crying is intense and they may be difficult to console, and they may pull away from those who remind them too much about the loved one.

If the dead one appears in dreams, they may become afraid and confused. More than children in other age-groups, they may respond by withdrawing from their surroundings. They are also more prone to play out the event, sometimes repeatedly.

But small children are also protected by their lack of a grasp of concepts and their reduced capacity to understand the long-term implications of events. The youngest ones may believe that the lost one will return, and we should not underestimate how this can help them in their grief. Younger children are also helped by their natural openness as well as their ability to be concrete and direct.

They often react to death with anxious attachment behaviour, with anxiety about strangers, crying, clinging, the need for much reassurance and so forth. Many become more difficult to steer and more angry than usual. Regressive behaviour, such as wetting and soiling, and sleep disturbances (nightmares) are also common. Although they seldom show sadness for long periods of time, they gradually develop their sadness span. They may lose interest in play, as well as masking their sadness and depression by acting-out behaviour such as temper tantrums.

School-age children

School-age children are in the process of decreasing their dependence on their parents, while they are increasing their contact with the world outside the family. This is done by going to school, and through taking part in activities outside the home. Importantly, they form friendships and relationships with members of society outside the inner family. They continue to form their identity, gain greater autonomy and greater control of their body.

Schoolchildren have a larger repertoire of coping strategies to meet and handle death and crisis situations. They are able to make inner plans of action that make them more 'invulnerable' (Pynoos and Eth 1984); they can think of things they will do to prevent such an event from happening again, as well as to undo what happened in their fantasies. They may fantasize that they called the ambulance, police or others, and that they can repair the damage. Also, in their fantasy or play they may take revenge on the one they hold responsible for what happened. Through changing, undoing, reversing or taking revenge, they can counteract feelings of helplessness.

At the same time we see that children may at this age suffer from additional problems because we demand more from them. They are to be strong, not cry, and so forth. Children's schoolwork may be affected because their spontaneous thoughts may be reduced and because intrusive images may lead to problems of concentration. A lowered mood can add to this reduction in thought activity.

Anxiety is a common reaction at this age, too. Guilt, identification with the lost person, different regressive behaviours, aggressive outbursts and depressive symptoms are also common. Isolation from peers, daydreaming and the inability to share feelings with adults and peers alike may also be present. Denial or suppression through various methods seems to increase with age.

Adolescence

In adolescence the developmental tasks are to gain greater autonomy, master the biological, psychological and social changes characteristic of this period, and to develop adult sexuality and the adult sexual role. Friends become even more important. Fear of rejection, ambivalence towards parents, and problems of dependence and independence are part of their life situation. Adolescence, with its increased independence of parents, involves maturing and learning in relation to loss and separation, and deaths may have a negative impact on this development.

A death can result in conflicts with parents and others, or in disturbances in the classroom, and adolescents may become more sexually active as a consequence of a loss. They may also be very judgemental of themselves, especially if they think they could have done more to prevent what happened. The magical thinking of earlier childhood is easily reactivated, and thus guilt feelings and self-reproach do not need an objective foundation to gain a foothold.

Their thought capacity enables them to abstract understanding of motivation, and alternative courses of action, and they may clearly see how the event has consequences for the rest of their life. The death of a close family member, especially the death of a parent, may sometimes be experienced as a stigma, something to be hidden, and something they are ashamed of. The intensity of feelings in adolescence may result in more repression of feelings, or in the avoidance of confrontation, and reactions may be expressed more through behaviour and conflicts with the environment.

Violent human-caused deaths may activate adolescents' own destructive fantasies and aggression:

> In a group of teenagers where a young man murdered his mother, many asked if this could happen in their family. Several wondered if they, in a given situation, could do something similar if they lost control. They became afraid of losing control of their own impulses.

In adolescence children also fear the loss of control over their emotions. This is most evident in boys who, as a result of a variety of influences, have learnt that feelings should not be openly expressed. Suppression of reactions and denial of death is not uncommon among adolescents. Some will seek out dangerous experiences where they gain a sense of control over death. Risk-taking behaviour interacts with increased fear in their parents, and may lead to confrontations on the home front.

Generally, children's attempt to master what has happened is a function of their age and maturity, even though there is some commonality in reactions across ages. With age, the ability to regulate strong feelings, and the ability to form inner plans of action that can decrease the fear of repetition, increases. Depending on age and maturity level, children will be differently affected by their families' reactions and external social pressure, as well as their own inner psychic conflicts. Unfortunately, we do not yet know enough about the interplay between trauma processing and the different developmental tasks of childhood.

The similarity between grief reactions in children and adults is striking. This is so for both grief- and crisis-responses. Leonore Terr (1979), in her study of a group of children who were held kidnapped, comments on this:

> Since the age span was five to fourteen years one would expect to find important differences in reactions on the basis of developmental stage. This was, surprisingly, not the case. There was a striking similarity in reactions over the age range. (Terr 1979, p.616)

Chapter Four

What makes the grief worse?

Several factors can make grief work more difficult.

Adults' handling of the death

First and foremost, the way adults handle the death can create problems for children. When facts are hidden, or the child is not properly informed about the circumstances and the cause of the death, fantasies may prevail. When a death is anticipated, adults often forget to update children about the course and prognosis of the disease, and children are thus badly prepared for the death, or have little understanding of what is going on.

By excluding the children from seeing the dead person or from participating in the funeral, by hiding their reactions from children, or by shutting the children out from the adult world in other ways, adults can make worse a situation that is already difficult for children.

Type of death

The type of death is another dimension that has an impact on children's grief reactions. For both adults and children alike, sudden deaths are more difficult to cope with. They leave no time for preparation on the mental level, and the child's sense of security in the world may be shattered. Such deaths have a stronger impact on the adult world, with consequences for how children's needs are handled. In addition, sudden deaths are often characterized by traumatic aspects that adults want to shield the child from. Children who witness their loved one's death are especially at risk and need to be monitored to secure early help should they develop post-traumatic problems.

Expected deaths lead to other strains that sometimes can be very hard for children. To wait for a possible death is in itself a stressful experience. Changes in the climate in the home; parents who worry if it is a sibling who is ill; crisis tops surrounding hospitalizations; hope and despair that varies; fear at returning from school and not knowing what can have happened in the meantime and so on, all will take their toll on children and parents. Children may be exposed to dramatic changes in the dying person as well as helplessness over not being able to do anything (Saldinger, Cain and Porterfield 2003). Research has shown that there are plenty of traumatic elements related to both children's and adults' illness, to such an extent that both the ill person and the family members can develop post-traumatic symptoms (Bruce 2006). Different stressors related to expected and unexpected deaths can therefore lead to comparable levels of stress for the remaining children.

As described before, the intensity and duration of the child's grief reactions will be related to who died, with parental death being the most disastrous for the child.

Relationship with the dead person

An ambivalent relationship with the deceased can complicate children's grief. This is the case when there has been strong jealousy of siblings, but also when a parent who has mal-treated or abused a child dies, or where other factors have led to a negative relationship between the dead person and the child. In such situations grief is mixed with relief at the absence of the dead person, often resulting in shame, self-reproach and ambivalent reactions. Where there has been violence in the home, children can experience intensified distress because they may have developed both somatic and psychological problems as a consequence of what they have experienced, not least because such a home environment led to problems in the attachment to others. A child's attachment history can determine grief reactions both in childhood and early adulthood (Stroebe, Schut and Stroebe 2005), and insecure or dismissive attachment increase the risk for com-plicated grief. For a child with insecure attachment even short separations from parents or caregivers can provoke strong reactions and fear of a new loss.

Support

The support the child receives varies greatly. Some have a family characterized by inner cohesion and commonality, while others live in chaotic homes, where children's needs can be low on the priority list when a death occurs. The support surrounding a child depends on the opportunities that the child is given to work through what has happened. It is not necessarily the size of the recovery environment that is most important, but the emotional climate surrounding the child following a death. After parental death a positive climate and interaction between children and the remaining parent, where the child is met with understanding and permission to talk about feelings without keeping anything back, is associ-ated with the least mental difficulties in the aftermath (Tein *et al.* 2006). When children's needs are accepted and they are helped to confront what has happened, the grief process will proceed more satisfactorily.

Access to a replacement person

Children's access to a replacement person can have an impact on their grief. Early access to the remaining parent or to another adult they trust following the loss of a parent can decrease the chance of unnecessary reactions. If the dead person had sole responsibility for the child, and it takes time to establish a close relationship with new carers, this may have negative consequences. Stability in providing for daily primary needs is important for the child. With regard to the loss of siblings, friends and so on, we have less information about the importance of substitute or replacement relationships. Siblings may sometimes demand that parents provide them with a new brother or sister, but sometimes they are not pleased with the replacement that arrives. With regard to love relationships among adolescents, we have even less knowledge of how such losses influence the establishment of new relationships. We do not know whether some of our knowledge of the consequences of the loss of a partner is relevant to pre-adolescents and adolescents.

Fantasies and causal thinking

Children's fantasies and causal thinking may have a negative influence on their grief. It is not uncommon for children to have two versions of what has happened. One is the official, built on the information they have received, and the other is built on their own fantasies about the event. The following example illustrates how fantasies can influence a child's reactions.

> Robert, age three, refused to be cared for by his mother following his 18-month-old sister's death. He only accepted

being cared for by his father. This became a big problem within the family. In a counselling session at the hospital the parents told how the mother had had to leave for the hospital in a hurry, and that Robert never saw his sister again. The boy thought his mother was responsible for his sister's death, and he was scared she would drive away with him also. In a session shortly thereafter, the parents brought the child to the hospital playroom where he was informed by a paediatrician of what happened to his sister at the hospital, and about how important it had been that his mother came to the hospital as quickly as possible. He was brought to the room where she had died, and received reassuring information about the difference between dangerous and non-dangerous illnesses. This reduced his fear, and soon afterwards things had normalized at home.

It is worth noting that some children have fantasies about the hospital being a place where children are sent to die or be killed. It takes no great imagination to understand children's confusion in this area, as they often hear about deaths taking place at hospitals. Following death as a result of disease, some children develop fantasies and misconceptions about illness and contagion. It is important for parents to be aware of this and to watch for signs of the child's understanding, to make sure that children are provided with information that counteracts any misconceptions.

Children's fantasies may also concern how the dead person looks, especially if the dead person was injured or first found after some time. Without a realistic basis, such fantasies may remain in a child's thoughts for a long time.

Personality and former experience

The child's personality and former experience may have an impact on grief work. Some children are more thoughtful and brooding, and may think about the death day in and day out. Some children face difficulties relatively easily; others more easily lose their foothold. Emotionally unstable children, and reclusive and isolated children, will experience difficulties in their grief more readily than more robust children. The level of emotional maturity may also have an influence. Unfortunately, we lack adequate information about children's ability to cope in such situations, but from clinical work we know that children's capacity to face life crises can vary greatly.

Previous experience may have a differential impact on how a child copes with such grief. Painful losses or separations that have never been properly worked through can make a child more vulnerable. If their first acquaintance with death was through a more distant relative or less well-known person's death, this may have increased the child's capacity for understanding, while the death of a parent as their first exposure to death is much more devastating. If the child has been shut out from the adult world in relation to an earlier death in the family, this may distinguish the demand and expectations they face adults with: 'I want to take part in my baby sister's funeral, because I was not allowed to go to my grandmother's funeral.'

In many respects it is true to say that dimensions which relate in different ways to adults' lack of acceptance and recognition of children's grief can seriously hamper children's long-term resolution of losses. In addition to better knowledge about children and grief within kindergartens and schools, the counselling and follow-up from healthcare workers have improved, and consequently children are met by a warmer, more caring climate. This may explain why the number of children that experience serious problems over time seem to be lower in newer compared to older studies, although this may also reflect better quality of the study methods.

Chapter Five

Sex differences
in children's grief

———▸———

In reading the literature on grief in children, it is surprising to see how little sex differences are mentioned. Many parents will spontaneously mention differences in this area. Their experience is that boys, more than girls, refrain from talking about the death and that they have difficulty showing their feelings. This does not necessarily mean all boys or only boys, but nevertheless it is common. The differences are more pronounced as children progress through school-age, and are particularly pronounced in adolescence. In a study we made of children's reactions to the murder of a schoolteacher, we found that girls acknowledged grief and crisis reactions to a much greater extent than boys (Dyregrov *et al.* 1994). The girls cried more, they experienced more difficulty concentrating, became more jumpy, anxious and so forth. Only in one area did the boys acknowledge more reactions (although not significantly so) than girls: they had to a greater degree tried to keep thoughts on what had happened away.

It was also disturbing to observe how the boys lacked the ability to express their feelings in writing. In answers to a short questionnaire, girls could write extensively about their first reactions, and about what had made the greatest impression on them, while the boys gave short answers and showed little ability to translate their feelings into words. Below are two representative examples of how a boy and a girl answered the question: 'Can you describe how you reacted when you first learnt what had happened?'

> *Boy*: 'I became shocked. I could not understand what had happened.'
> *Girl*: 'I did not believe it was true, I became very shocked. Then I cried for a while, but still did not believe it was true. My reaction came when we had a memorial service at the school. It was painful when it lasted, but felt good afterward because you were allowed to cry.'

It was also striking that when we compared the three affected classes in the ninth grade, it was the boys in the class who had had the teacher as their primary teacher who described their reaction with the fewest words.

Also, regarding support from the environment, boys and girls differed. Almost all the girls had a good friend in whom they could confide and who had been of support, while less than 40% of the boys reported the same. In addition, girls had talked more about the event at home than had the boys. Even though this was not a comprehensive and well-controlled study, it gives a clear impression that boys, to a much lesser extent than girls, acknowledge grief and crisis reactions, and that boys, to a lesser extent than girls, process such situations through the help of words.

Gender differences are also reflected in other studies where it is common that girls report more reactions than boys. In one of the few studies that has followed children over an extended period of time (20 years) after the loss of a parent, the risk of developing major depression in adult age was only increased among women (Reinherz *et al.* 1999). There are also many more girls than boys who develop post-traumatic stress disorder (PTSD). We might think that because girls talk more with others, put their feelings into words more easily and so on, they should be better equipped to deal with trauma and loss, but this does not seem to be the case.

The reasons for such differences are probably various. Boys and girls differ in their play and friendships. Girls play more in pairs, two and two together; their play is more expressive, and their play centres on close human relationships (Lever 1976). Through their play they build up a language for feelings. Boys' play focuses more on learning their role in the group, how to stick to rules and not show feelings. Social learning and upbringing is also different for the two sexes, and in many ways this makes boys more helpless in relation to their own feelings. Through active and passive learning they are taught to suppress and deny their feelings (with the exception of aggression) in many areas of life. It is possible, though speculative, that through evolution the two sexes have developed different ways of coping with death and danger. Boys and men seem to suppress events more easily, lay them behind themselves and look to the future, while girls and women to a larger degree cope by confronting their feelings. Professionals in the grief area believe that the explanation for girls' stronger reactions must be sought in the fact that they are more sensitive for stress in the family, are more concerned about family members (i.e. remaining parent) and feel more responsibility within the family:

> Kristin's mother committed suicide when Kristin was 16. She lived with her father and one brother of 14. She felt that the mother was the glue in the family, the one that bound them together. She felt obliged to take on some of the mother's tasks in securing family rituals such as the joint dinner every day. A family conversation about the burdens she felt over time made it obvious that the two male family members did not prioritize these functions as highly as Kristin.

The access girls develop to their feelings during childhood also makes them 'closer' to their feelings, and taken together this may explain the gender differences.

Regardless of the reasons for such differences, it is important to be aware that they exist. Unfortunately, our help is much more tailored to girls' ways of reacting than to boys', as most of the help centres on using conversations and words. For many boys it is less natural to express their emotional experience in words, and they can more easily do this through concrete activities (Chapter Eight includes a short presentation of such methods).

Taken together, research indicates that it is girls that are more vulnerable following the death of a loved one. It also means that parents may lower their shoulders somewhat when it comes to the anxiety that is easily triggered when boys do not want to talk about what happened. This is just not a coping method so often used by boys. It is only if boys withdraw from usual activities, their behaviour changes a lot or they do not function in school, that parents should be concerned.

Chapter Six

Care for children in grief and crisis

Children's grief work encompasses both the cognitive and emotional working-through of what has happened. The guidelines described below try to stimulate both dimensions of this grief work. A short summary of the guidelines may be found in the Appendix.

Counselling the parents

Perhaps the most important help that parents can give their children is to care adequately for themselves, so that their own reluctance to confront what has happened does not impede the child's grief work. It is therefore important for parents to ensure their own working-through of what has happened. To be able to meet children's needs, it is necessary to acquire information about children's reactions, be prepared for their questions and to get advice on how best to care for the children.

Parents' grief can be difficult and hard, and children in a family that is struck by loss cannot expect parents to show them the same attention as usual. How difficult this situation can be is illustrated by the following words from a mother who lost her daughter six months after her birth:

My seven-year-old son kept asking many questions about the death of his infant sister. I tried to answer as best as I could, but it was not easy. I kept thinking that I had so many questions myself, questions that nobody could answer for me. Sometimes I got mad at him for asking, but mostly I ignored him. One day he entered the kitchen and said he pitied me for always having to do the dishes. He asked me if I wanted a hug, because he loved me so much. It felt good, but hurt at the same time. I felt guilty. Instead of being glad for what he said, I thought that I would never hear my daughter say the same thing. Then I felt so stupid, and more guilty. How could I let my lost daughter mean more to me than him, when I have him and he needs me? I hugged him, and I cried. But more, he has me again, and I'm accepting the loss better.

By entering bereavement groups or by seeking professional counselling, parents can get the help they need to be better able to care for their children. Those who seek more information about grief reactions in adults should consult the following literature: regarding the loss of a child, Rando (1986), Riches and Dawson (2000), Rosenblatt (2000); regarding the loss of a parent, Worden (1996); regarding the loss of a sibling, Dyregrov and Dyregrov (2005); Hogan and DeSantis (1996); regarding the loss of a partner and other losses, Rando (1984, 1988), Parkes and Weiss (1983), Neimeyer (2000) and Stroebe, Stroebe and Hansson (1993). Maybe the most thorough and insightful book about human reactions to loss, with a special focus on grief in children, is John Bowlby's book *Attachment and Loss* (1980).

Presenting children with the news of a death

Presenting the news of a death in the family to a child should preferably be carried out by the child's parents, or by someone else who is emotionally close to the child. Sometimes this task falls on a teacher or other adult. When a child is to be told, the setting should, if possible, be chosen with care. The child needs some time to prepare mentally for what is coming. That means that one does not dump the news on the child, but finds the time to sit down, go to a suitable room and so forth. The news should be formulated in a direct manner. This can, for example, be done in the following way: 'I have something sad to tell you. An accident has happened. It involved your daddy. There was an explosion at his work site, and he was seriously hurt. Even though the ambulance and health personnel quickly arrived and did everything they could to save his life, there was nothing they could do. From what we have learned the damages were so extensive that they think he died almost instantaneously.'

Such messages must contain the facts that are known. It is very important that this information is correct, and if we are unsure, the information must be checked. Children's immediate reaction to the news can vary greatly, but adults must be prepared for reactions as variable as loud denial and active protest, or crying and despair. This is why it is important that the setting (the place) for breaking the news is such that it allows for the multitude of reactions that children may show. The situation must also allow for time to sit uninterrupted with the child afterwards. If the child denies the news, this is a sign that it cannot be taken in all at once, and that the child needs time. Then it can be helpful to say: 'I understand that it is difficult for you to understand that this has really happened to your brother, but I am sorry to say it is so.' This does not add to the denial, but at the same time shows that the reaction is accepted. Frequently, everything has to be repeated several times during the first day.

Even though the immediate reaction may be crying and despair, the child may, after some minutes, stop crying and ask adequate questions such as: 'Where did they find him?' or

'What do they think happened?' If the child cries intensely, it is important that he or she is allowed to do so, and that adults do not try to make them stop too soon simply because they may find it so hard to listen to. Nobody should say that the child should pull him- or herself together and stop crying. It is better to put a comforting arm around the child while he or she is allowed to react.

It is a clear advantage to be able to be concrete in breaking the news. Especially with regard to younger children, it is important not to use such euphemisms as 'sleep' and 'journey', as well as abstract concepts such as 'the soul'. Such explanations reinforce a non-biological understanding and create confusion and fear for others who are on a journey or asleep. Concrete explanations such as: 'Your sister is dead. Her heart has stopped beating; she does not breathe any more; her hair has stopped growing, and she can feel no pain' will help the child to process the event on the cognitive level.

Children's participation in rituals

In Western societies we have gradually used fewer and fewer rituals. Especially in relation to death there has been a decrease in the use of ritual; 'the funeral has taken place in silence', 'please do not make condolences'. It is important to remember that rituals have important functions for us. They help us make the unreal real, they counteract fantasies, they stimulate grief work and allow us the opportunity to express our grief symbolically. They also symbolize the transition between life and death, they allow us to bid farewell and they stimulate the expression of emotions. But perhaps more important, they structure a 'chaotic' situation. We should also remember that the rituals are not only for the bereaved, but allow others the opportunity to show their concern, support and attention. These are dimensions we tend to forget in our eagerness to do things simply and with the least amount of distress (see Rando 1985 for a presentation of therapeutic rituals).

Many adults fear that they will lose control during the rituals. They fear that they will break down; fear they will start to cry; fear what other people will say; fear that they will be hysterical and fear meeting other people. This often leads to the use of tranquillizers to get through the situation and to cutting short the rituals. Unfortunately, this fear of the hurt and of eventual strong reactions also includes fear of hurting the children. Adults therefore have a tendency to exclude children from the adult world when it comes to the rituals.

But children have just as great a need as adults to make the unreal real, and to gain a concrete basis for their grief rather than fantasies. Children need to be part of the ritual of seeing the dead, and to be present at the funeral ceremony, to make sure that their grief work is given the same basis or opportunity as adults', so as not to reinforce children's denial of the death. Children need to know that the dead body will be buried or burnt to ashes.

But, when including children, it must be ensured that this will not stress the children in an unnecessary way. Many adults are against including children in such situations, because they have negative memories going back to their own childhood. This can be the result of being reprimanded for not showing enough respect, or because they were thrown into the position of seeing a loved one without preparation. Sometimes children demand that they are part of the rituals:

> Eleven-year-old Peter told his parents he wanted to see his stillborn sister. He had seen his grandmother following her death, and now he wanted to make sure he also got to see his sister.

> Nine-year-old Susan was not at home when her parents took her sister to the hospital where she died shortly thereafter. She demanded to see her sister, because it was so strange and sad that she suddenly was gone, and that she never should see her again.

Sometimes children can become bitter when they are excluded:

> Nine-year-old Greg was very disappointed about not getting to see his mother following her death. He was at the hospital when the adults got to see her, but no one offered him the opportunity to participate. His father did not have enough knowledge about his needs, and did not know children were allowed to take part on such occasions. Later, Greg's father said this was something that the personnel at the hospital should have informed him of.

If children are to participate in seeing the dead and in the funeral, certain guidelines should be followed:

- the child must be prepared
- the child must be accompanied by a trusted adult
- the child must be given the opportunity to work through his or her impressions.

Proper preparation

Before a child is taken in to see the dead person, he or she must be properly prepared. This means that the child should be given a description of what the room will look like, that is, the colour of the rugs and walls, how the room is decorated, whether there are flowers, candles and so on, and how the casket is arranged, that is, where it stands, its colour, ornaments and so forth. The child also needs to be told how the dead person is lying: 'He is lying in a nice white casket, dressed in a white shirt. His hands are folded over his chest. His skin looks different from usual. It is more white with blue dots' and so forth. It is important that an adult first enters the room to see the dead person and then comes back to describe how he or she is different from usual. The preparation must include the special sensory impressions that a child faces in this situation: that the body will be cold on touch, what they will see, and smells if there are any. It is not uncommon that the hair can be combed in another direction than usual, something that can etch itself into memory:

> His hair was combed directly backwards. He never had his hair like that. I was shocked and see the image in front of me when I go to bed at night. (Boy, 11)

> She was much whiter than they said. Nobody told me this. (Girl, 12)

If the casket is half-closed this should be explained to the child, as many younger children do not realize or believe that the dead person's legs are inside the casket. Some children need the bottom part of the casket opened so that they can look inside to make sure for themselves that the legs are in there.

By taking time for this procedure, mental preparation is allowed and the situation becomes less of a shock. At the same time the formation of intrusive images is counteracted.

Children also need to be prepared for adults' reactions during these rituals, as they can be scared of strong overt emotional reactions. If they are prepared, and understand why adults react as they do, this problem is greatly reduced. But the strength of adult reactions can be frightening just the same:

> A girl of 16 said that the strongest part of the experience was to see her parents totally dissolved following her brother's death in an accident. That they who always had seemed so strong could break down so totally was very

frightening for her. Afterwards she was careful not to expose them to her own reactions.

Both before a 'viewing' and before the funeral, children should know what will happen, and what the room or chapel will look like. This includes the decorations, speeches given, singing or other things. It may also be useful for them to know 'how this will be for them'. How does it feel to be present and what reactions can they expect themselves? Without frightening them, they can be told that they probably will feel sad, somewhat anxious or overwhelmed by the atmosphere in the room or church.

As adults we ought to include children in decisions concerning the funeral when they reach school age. They often have clear opinions on what clothes the person should have on:

> 'My father was a caps-man,' a 12-year-old stated, and insisted that his father should wear a cap in the coffin in addition to a vest he always used.

Why does the dead person lie in white linens? Children might want their dead brother or sister to wear clothes that they were particularly fond of. They may also have a clear opinion about the music that should accompany the ritual. Why should we not listen to them? When children get to choose clothes or musical pieces, the ritual will be more personal for them, and it may counteract the helplessness they may feel. Children may harbour wishes that are important to them regarding these rituals, wishes that we as adults may not know about if we do not try to include them in the planning of the rituals.

Company of a trusted adult

The child must be accompanied through the ceremonies by a trusted adult. When he or she has lost a parent, sibling or grandparent, this person does not have to be the parents or remaining parent, but somebody else close to the child. This helps the parents to participate fully in the rituals without having to divide their attention between their child and the ritual. The adult that accompanies the child should, apart from being a trusted person, be someone who can explain what is happening, who can support and console, and who can follow the child outside if needed.

Concrete expressions of grief

Children are concrete, and need to give concrete expressions to their grief. This means that the child should be encouraged to bring something they can put in or on the casket. This can be a letter, a drawing, flower(s) or a toy that they especially associate with the dead person, for example the toy they played with the last time they were together. This helps children to bid farewell, and it gives grief a concrete expression. When a death occurs suddenly, children just as adults are deprived of the opportunity to bid farewell to the dead person. Often they think of all they would have wanted to say to the deceased. By asking: 'What would you have said if you had known that it was the last time you would speak to…?' and then asking them to write this in a letter or whisper it inside their head or into the ear of the dead person, this can to some extent compensate for the farewell they never got to make.

In such situations details can be very important. Younger children may insist that the flower or drawing should be placed in such a way that the dead person can 'see' it, and not at the other end of the casket. With small children we must remember that they need to be lifted up to see the dead person properly, and that their perspective is quite unsatisfactory if they only get a glimpse of the person from their standpoint. By taking pictures or a video film the possibility for children to return to the situation later when they seek more clarity or information is kept, in addition to the use it can have later for children too young to take this in or children entering the family at a later stage.

Both children and adults sometimes need to be given 'permission' to touch, hold, kiss or hug the dead person. Often family members think the deceased is the 'property' of the hospital or the church, and that it is prohibited to touch. Afterwards they may say that they had so much wanted to touch, but did not dare. Children can be given permission for this contact – it is not dangerous, and may reduce the unreality of the death. At the same time it is important that they are not pressured, and we should know that there is a short space between what is helpful and therapeutic, and what can be traumatic if adults are not able to prepare children well enough, or the context surrounding the situation is not well enough planned or thought through. Sometimes adolescents need some time alone with the deceased. As they seldom ask for this themselves, asking about this must be the adults' responsibility.

Parents must be prepared for children's reactions during these rituals. Young children especially may sometimes shock adults. They can put their fingers into the mouth or nose of the deceased, or push open his or her eyelid. This is a child's way of checking out what this 'dead' is, and comparing it with sleep. Many parents have experienced young children examining them in a similar way if they are asleep or lie with their eyes closed.

Smaller children can also be very active, and may have difficulty sitting still, so much so that adults feel that it shows lack of respect for the solemn occasion, and that they do not have the quiet atmosphere that it deserves. Often, though, children become more quiet than usual, because there are so many impressions to take in. Although adults must be tolerant of children's behaviour, there is no need for younger children to stay in the room as long as the parents. They can leave after a while, and leave the parents (or remaining parent) with the time and peace they need to bid a respectful farewell.

Viewing the body

If the dead person is badly injured, children are often excluded from the viewing ceremony. This is also why many adults refrain from viewing the body. Our experience is that there should be very extensive disfigurement to the body before adults or children should be discouraged from viewing. The bereaved are less concerned with the injuries than with the recognizable parts of the body. For example, parents whose severely malformed babies die shortly following birth often centre their attention on details that make the baby 'part of the family', such as 'he's got my jaw' or 'look how similar her eyes are to mine'.

Because the unreality of the situation is greater following sudden deaths, and because fantasies can be vivid in such cases, it is particularly important to see the body after such deaths. It is easier to handle *one* concrete image than changing fantasies such as 'maybe it was not him', or 'how bad she must have looked since we were not allowed to see her'. I have frequently arranged meetings between the bereaved and emergency medical workers or hospital personnel who saw the dead person, in order to let them tell the bereaved who did not see the body what he or she looked like. It is my experience that children and adults seldom regret viewing the body, while those who do not can regret this for years afterwards. If the injuries are very severe, parts of the body may have to be covered.

There are, of course, situations where the bereaved should not be encouraged to view the body, because of its condition.

If they demand to see the body anyway, and it is possible, they should not be prevented from doing so. Then we have to prepare them as fully as possible for the situation, and make sure they receive adequate follow-up.

There is some research indicating that children may show an increase in behavioural problems if they enter into rituals without preparation or proper support in the situation (McCown 1984; Poijula et al. 2001b). Throughout the years I have been referred quite a few children who have been bothered by the image of their lost loved one as they saw him or her in the coffin, even though they were relatively well prepared. Most often this has been caused by a sensory impression, from the look on the face, the hair combed in the wrong direction, the colour of the face, the damages to the body, the marks from the rope around the throat and so on, which has etched itself into memory, returning as intrusive recollections. For some it was the coldness when touching the body with resulting problems touching cold things that prompted the remittance.

> Brian (aged eight) saw his mother following her sudden death from an overdose. He was well prepared but due to her personal problems his relationship to her was not only positive. Three weeks after the death his father brought him to see me because he slept very poorly and had intrusive images from viewing his mother. He drew a dark, angry face and told me that he constantly saw this while at school and when he went to bed at night. The mother looked much darker in the face during the viewing than he had expected. He was helped through a trauma-specific method where he learned to control the image that bothered him, alongside learning distraction methods that could assist him when he did not want to think of his mother. When he came back some weeks later, he was no longer bothered by the images

and warmed a psychologist's heart by saying: 'I hope I can have you as a friend.'

Although there is a risk that such situations can create traumatic memories, I will not advise against including children. The trauma-specific methods that have been developed in later years means that such memories can be alleviated. However, we cannot repair the damage we can cause by excluding children and preventing their chance to take farewell during such rituals. The traumatizing potential in the situation should, however, make us acutely aware of using enough time in preparing children for participation.

Conversation and playing out impressions

Allowing time for conversation about the event, or time to play out impressions afterwards, is important for children after the ceremonies. This means that adults have to make room for, stimulate and accept this in the child. Children's expressive means will vary with age. The most important thing that adults can do is to let the child work through and get a grip on his or her impressions by tumbling around with them in words or play.

Participation in the funeral

Sometimes the child does not want to see the dead person or take part in the funeral. The child should never be forced to participate. But, on the other hand, we must not accept no for an answer too early. In the same way as adults, children can be frightened by such situations, and hesitate. By taking time with the children and explaining to them what will happen and why it is important that they participate, their immediate resistance can be overcome. But again, children must never be forced.

Most often, when children do not take part in these rituals, it is because the adults cannot accept having the children present. This must be respected, but again it is important to take time with the parents to explain the importance of children's participation, and explain how experience of similar situations has clearly shown that children cope better when they are allowed to participate. If health personnel or clergy take time for such guidance, a better basis is formed for the parents' decision. If parents still cannot face having the children included in the ceremonies, they can inform the children thoroughly afterwards:

> Helen (three years of age) was given the following description by her mother of how her father had looked: 'I have been and seen your daddy, seen that he was dead. We will never see him again, never talk with him again. He looked very peaceful in the white, nice casket he was lying in. The casket had gold at the edges and he had a nice silk coverlet on, with nice flowers sewn into it. He looked so nice.' Some days afterwards, Helen went with her mother to his grave. There she was very occupied by which way he was lying, where the head was, and she also thought that he must be very dirty. Her mother had to explain that there was a lid on the casket, that it was not open as with Snow White's casket, which her mother had told her about. She also wanted to help her dad out of the casket, and she wondered when he was coming home.

Cremation

If the body is to be cremated, this can be hard for parents to explain to children. For smaller children who see death as a temporary condition, burning can be misunderstood and seen as something that will prevent the dead person from returning. Usually it is easier for children to accept this than it is for adults. It can be explained to children that when something is dead it will decay, and that a cremation will turn a body that no longer feels anything into ashes.

Sometimes children are interested in the details surrounding the cremation. This can be hard for parents to deal with. Where the ash is kept can also be a subject of questions. Most parents find that the best way to handle children's questions is to be direct and open, and to take time to answer them thoroughly. Children with a religious background are less worried about this aspect, as they are familiar with the concept that it is only the 'empty shell' (body) that is burned, while the soul has gone to heaven.

The multicultural world we live in makes it important to acknowledge the cultural differences when arranging for children's participation. In parts of Africa they believe that the soul of a living person who comes too close to a deceased person risks following the dead person, and children are believed to need special protection. It is evident that with such beliefs the inclusion of children in rituals after death, which is advocated here, will be in conflict with parents' belief. In other cultures information about a father's death during war is kept from children because it is believed to be the best for the children based on the assumption of children as innocent and incapable of managing this information. We should not force our own cultural customs or rituals on families with a different cultural background, but at the same time we should not just bend backwards and think that the culture is always right (Dyregrov *et al.* 2002). Globally there seems to be a development towards more understanding and inclusion of children, often carried forward by women, and we can explain to parents with a different cultural background from our own why we think it is important to be open, direct and concrete in our communication about death, and why we include children in different rituals.

Chapter Seven

Guidelines for taking care of children's needs

Open and direct communication

Trying to keep information about a death away from children usually has negative consequences. Children want to and need to learn the truth, although it must be put in words suitable for their age. Illness and death must be explained openly, truthfully and directly, without euphemisms that can lead to confusion and fear. For smaller children, it is important to refrain from abstract explanations. If concepts such as heaven, God and Jesus have not been part of the child's daily world, introducing them in relation to a current death is not the right time. This might be an easy way out for adults, but for children it means that they have to struggle to merge the abstract and the concrete, with resulting confusion.

Where religious concepts are part of the everyday life of the child, however, it can be appropriate to use them. Even the most 'ungodly' adult often mobilizes concepts about a life after death and a future reunification when they have to talk to children about death. It is also common among a majority of children, regardless of them being religious or not, to have conceptions of an afterlife from where the dead can keep an eye on them (Landsdown, Frangoulis and Jordan 1997). If a religious solution is chosen, it is best to use simple ideas. It is better to say, 'God will look after your baby sister' than 'God loved your sister so much that he took her up to heaven'.

By giving children concrete and direct information, fantasies and confusion are avoided. Often, adults refrain from telling children about a death because they think that they cannot tolerate the truth, or they keep parts of what happened from the children for the same reason. Most often we do this because we ourselves have difficulty telling them, and this is an excuse for not having to undertake unpleasant adult tasks. Children are usually quite capable of meeting reality openly and directly. Problems in understanding arise because adults underestimate children's abilities.

By giving children information in a direct and open fashion, we also prevent children from accidentally learning about aspects of the event from their social surroundings. If this happens, it can seriously shake the trust they have in parents or adults:

> After a father's sudden death at home an eight- and an 11-year-old came to a session together with their mother. The mother and the children clearly held different memories about what had happened, with the children agreeing and a somewhat different version from the mother. There was obviously a need for integrating the facts in a manner they could agree on. In addition, it emerged that the mother in an almost mysterious way had kept from the children what cremation meant and had explained that the coffin and the body turned to ashes without flames. Both children had disbelief regarding information coming from the mother, and it became necessary with a conversation with the mother alone to stress the importance of communicating directly, openly and truthfully with the children. The explanation of the cremation that she had provided could easily be dismissed if the children talked with others about it. A very concrete book by a Danish psychologist that

shows pictures of the cremation oven and so on, was very helpful in talking with these children (Jacobsen 1989).

Not only should information be open and direct, but it should be immediate. Delay in giving the child important information can, besides reducing trust in adults, increase the chance that they learn about what happened in an unplanned situation. Of course adults may need some time to collect themselves before telling children, but delaying giving information can have negative consequences:

> Andrew (14) received a text message from a good friend that his brother had been involved in a serious traffic accident and was believed to be dead. The friend had recognized his car. The parents wanted to wait before telling him until they knew more, and he sat waiting for them to call for a very, very long time.

If we have to use a 'white' lie, or only tell part of the truth to the child, we should try to correct this early: 'I did not tell you the whole truth yesterday because the situation was so new and shocking to me, it became too much. I will try to make it up now, by telling you everything I know.' Sometimes it is not easy to repair well-meaning acts from adults:

> A father took his own life while the mother was away and her two daughters, both below 11 years of age, were visiting another family. The priest that came to tell them what had happened told them that the gun had gone off by accident. The problem was that a cousin knew what had really happened, and had conveyed this to others. The mother understood that she was in haste to tell the truth and she told them openly (assisted by a psychologist) that the information they got from the priest about the gun going off by accident was not totally correct; the father had shot himself. 'Then the priest lied', the eldest daughter said at once. The mother tried to explain how the priest had done this with

the best intentions, but the next remark from the girl made it obvious that the lost trust was total: 'I looked him in the eyes and asked him, "Is it true what you say?" and he answered, "yes".'

Research shows that children who experience that parents are open in their communication in the home, experience less depression and anxiety following the death of a parent (Raveis *et al.* 1999).

Usually, it is best not to let others give the information. It is best for children to learn what is to be learnt from parents, even though it might be somewhat discontinuous and incomplete. Regardless of how it is being told, it needs to be repeated, to ensure that the child has understood what has been said, and to allow follow-up questions. Sometimes people in our social surroundings may react negatively toward this openness:

> A mother chose to tell her seven-year-old daughter about the situation of her seriously ill (dying) infant brother, and about the chances of a permanent handicap if he, against expectation, should survive. This resulted in the visit of a neighbour who told her frankly that such things should not be said to a child.

When explaining death to preschool children we should keep in mind what was written earlier about how their understanding of death is not fully developed. A suitable explanation would be:

> 'Mama will explain what death is. When you and I are eating, and you go to kindergarten and I go to work, it is because our body lives. When we live it is because our body has a heart, lungs and a stomach that makes the body alive. The heart pumps blood in the body, and the blood transports what we need to live around the body. The stomach takes what we eat and makes it useful for the body, and the

lungs use the air we breathe to help the body live. When Mama says that Daddy is dead, it means that the accident (illness) has made the heart stop beating, and therefore he cannot live any longer. Now that he is dead he cannot breathe any more, his hair and nails have stopped growing, and he cannot feel any pain. When Daddy is dead, he does not need to drink or eat any more. This is a little difficult for you to understand, but Mama will explain it to you several times, and you may ask Mama questions if there is anything you wonder about.'

Death following an illness

When someone is seriously ill, with a deteriorating prognosis, children's need for updated information about the progress of the disease and its prognosis are often forgotten. Many children have difficulties understanding what illness, treatment and change in the condition over time means (Christ *et al.* 1993), and they need an explanation of what is happening, what is going to happen and why it happens. They may also need an explanation of what symptoms are caused by the disease and what result from the treatment (such as hair loss). Children can sense the change in emotional climate at home, as well as the reduced physical capacities of the ill person, and they need updated information that helps them to understand what is going on. Adolescents say that they want more information than they receive in information folders related to parents' diseases, and they want to know what websites they can visit (Forrest *et al.* 2006). If such information contains the certainty that there is a great risk of losing a loved one, a child can start his or her grief reactions before the death takes place. Children frequently go through a form of anticipatory grief:

Mary (11) knew her father was ill, and she had visited him at the hospital. She often asked when her dad would return from the hospital. One day her mother answered that he might not return, and why that was so. The next day she drew a graveyard with two graves (she had lost a sister some years before), a cross and a priest, and on the graves she wrote her sister's and her father's name. The mother thought this was alarming, but soon understood that this was her child's way of coping with what she just had learnt about her father's condition.

There is no recipe for how to tell a child that someone will die. Often children understand this long before the parents think they have understood – and unfortunately many adults delay telling the children until the children learn about it from others or until they have had to live with their fantasies for a while. Children can sometimes ask very directly. A direct way of telling them is:

> 'Mama's disease has become worse. It is difficult for her to eat, breathe and be awake. The doctors give her medicine to prevent her from having pain. They have tried everything they can to stop the disease, but now there is no more they can do. One day, and this day may not be far away, your mama will die. Then we all will be sad and long for her. But she will feel no pain, because we do not feel pain when we are dead.' If the child is religious we may add: 'Mama's body will be dead, but her soul will go to heaven.'

Parents have to tell children early about what they expect to happen. If the disease is life-threatening and the prognosis bad, the child should be told that even though the doctors will do all they can to make him or her well, it is not certain he or she will become better. Even though it is important to retain some hope until the end, children should not be given false expectations to ease the pain. But there are 'steps' in this process: a sick person can have a life-threatening disease without being ill (a person with cancer can go downhill-skiing); there are situations without much hope; there are situations where one frantically clings to a straw of hope; and, finally, there is the situation where the patient is dying. Swedish researchers have shown that no parents who spoke openly with their dying children before death have regretted their open communication, while 27% of those who did not speak openly with their child have since regretted this and been bothered by what they did (Kreicbergs *et al.* 2004). Although we do not have similar studies where one of the parents is dying, there is reason to believe that openness within the family will be the best foundation for children's coping, both while the parent is alive and after their death.

If it is a parent who is dying, continuity in the child's daily life is important. They need to be assured that there will always be someone there to take care of them. When a parent dies, it is also important that the child is able to spend time with his or her mother or father in the last phase of life, and that they are assured that the doctors will prevent any pain. In many hospitals care for children is an integrated part of family assistance. However, in other hospitals children are still excluded from the situation in a way that precludes a proper leave-taking. In the last hours of life, the hospital should allow children to stay with their dying mother or father, and make it easy for them to spend the night at the hospital if necessary.

We have not adequately looked at children as part of the bereaved family. Both parents should, if the parent's condition allows, be counselled on how to talk with their children, and on how children and adults can be together in the final hours of a parent's life. It is important that this process is not started when the dying person is too sick to participate. Most cancer societies provide information on the internet that can assist parents in caring for their children, as do other support organizations for other serious diseases.

It must be pointed out that death from illness differs from case to case, and some of the goals that have been mentioned here cannot be realized. But often it is old routines and lack of knowledge about children's needs that set limits, rather than the condition of the patient.

To some extent children can help in caring for their ill parent. The child should not be given too much responsibility or be overburdened, but be able to assist and be helpful, see and understand, and be close to their dying mother or father. There is no easy balance in such situations, because children at the same time need to live as normally as possible with play and activities adjusted to their age level. When ill parents or siblings have to stay in hospital for extended periods of time, some children refuse to go to visit or spend much time there. It is understandable that children want to shield themselves from the pain it means to visit their loved one in the hospital and as adults we can encourage, but not pressure, the child to visit. After the death adults need to refrain from comments that may increase a child's eventual bad conscience, but be willing to talk with the child about their misgivings in this regard.

Making the loss real

Different ceremonies and rituals help us to get a grip on what has happened, to understand that it really has happened and to confront the loss. Children have the same need as adults to get a grip on the event, and ritual acts or ceremonies are important in their grief work. Practically, this means that the child must be included in the adult ceremonies. This should follow the guidelines presented in Chapter Six.

Making the unreal real is also stimulated by keeping the memories of the deceased person present and visible, as part of the child's daily surroundings. Gradually the children and parents can remove those things that it would be unnatural to keep present. The clearing of the dead person's belongings is an activity the children should be part of. It is both painful and good to participate in this, but it is a natural part of the mourning process. The tempo in the clearing of things belonging to the deceased can vary within a family:

> In a family where a six-year-old was killed in an accident, the clearing away of his things had clearly gone too fast for his older brother of 12. When the family was asked what they had done with his things he very quickly said: 'The toothbrush shall remain in the bathroom!'

To talk within the family about what should happen with the deceased's clothes, personal computer and other possessions can avoid conflicts because someone gets something that another member thinks he or she should have. Siblings especially can react strongly if clothes that they strongly associate with their dead sibling are given to someone they regard as lower in the grief hierarchy than themselves:

> Mary was 15 when her older brother died in an accident. He had had a girlfriend for the last two months and her parents gave this girlfriend his favourite shirt. Mary reacted with strong anger mixed with a lot of tears. Why should this girlfriend that only had known him for two months get this shirt instead of her, whom had known him all his life!

It is not uncommon to observe parents and other adults hiding their feelings from their children. They may enter another room to prevent their children from seeing them cry, or they may hold their emotions back until the children have gone to bed. Sometimes they refrain from talking about the dead person because they think that this will only make things worse for the child. Hiding emotions from children can have negative effects: we then teach our children that feelings are to be kept to oneself, and we become a negative role model for our children. At the same time children can think that their caretakers have forgotten the lost one, and they experience an emotional climate in which they do not dare to express or talk about their feelings. Their grief has to be 'hidden'. Sometimes children leave clear signs of this, as when parents find pictures and albums out of order, a clear sign that the child had to 'steal' a look at them, as if they were not allowed to do so.

On the basis of adults' reluctance to talk with children about death, and the fact that adolescents often seek out friends to talk to, it is perhaps not so strange that adolescents who have lost a parent often say they have received better help from friends than parents.

If parents show continuous strong feelings, there may come a point when they have to 'pull themselves together', for example if they cry all the time. If a parent cannot talk about the dead person at all without strong feelings breaking through, the child may benefit from contact with another adult that the child can talk to, such as a teacher, counsellor or good friend of the family. Usually it will be best for children if adults are able to explain in words why they react as they do, to prevent the child from making up fantasies about this.

If a sibling has died, frequently children will reflect on whether his or her parents would have been equally sad if they had died. They need reassurance that their 'value' to the parents is as high as the child who died.

Often children try to protect and support their parents:

'Don't be sad, Mama, remember you have me.'

'Grandma, if you think that my sister will die, please do not tell Mama, because she will be so sad.'

Children can be of great support in such situations, and we should allow them to show that they care and acknowledge that it feels good that they think about us. At the same time the children's concern can be a signal to take more time to explain our feelings to them, to explain that it is permissible to be sad, and that when we feel sad, angry or tired this reflects how much we loved the one who died. By giving voice to our feelings, we give them learning for life. This helps them in building a register of feelings and a coping ability they can use when they face difficulties and crises later in life. Sometimes strong and lasting grief in parents can 'free' the children in a way: 'They carried the grief.'

Give time for cognitive mastery

Children build their understanding about what happened by questions, conversation and play:

> 'What does the baby get to drink down in the grave?'

> 'Which way is she lying in the casket?'

> 'Will his hair continue to grow?'

Questions are repeated and show that the child's mastery of the different aspects of the death is developed gradually. It is as if, for every time they ask, another piece of the puzzle is added and the piece is looked at repeatedly. Both parents' and other adults' patience can be stretched in a situation where there is a lack of energy. It is, however, important that children are allowed to ask these questions, that they are given time to grasp what has happened and that they do not have to base their understanding on fantasies, with the uncertainty and anxiety this can lead to.

The questions are often penetrating and painful for parents and adults. They go to the core of what it is hard for adults to look in the face:

> 'Are you sure we will never see him again?'

> 'Is Mama sitting up in heaven looking down at us?'

> 'Is it cold down in the grave?'

> 'Now Carly is dead, I want her bedroom.'

'Let's throw away his toothbrush, he doesn't need it any more.'

Carers have to be 'mentally prepared' for such questions and the thoughts that children tumble around with. If you do not have the answer to a child's question, it is best to say so, and if the question 'hurts', and you need time to think about the answer, just say: 'It hurts to talk about this right now. Let me think about it and then I will answer you later.'

Through counselling the adult carers, the child's network can be motivated and prepared for his or her reactions, and be able to provide better care.

When we talk to children about death, we must also be aware that such conversations will usually be rather short. Children let us in for a short while, and then they change the subject or say 'I am going out to play'. This is especially so for younger children, but even adolescents can shy away from longer conversations. We must remember that children are less tolerant of strong feelings than adults, that they have a shorter sadness span. Language is the primary mean of communication for adults more than for children, who may choose other forms of expression.

Sometimes children refuse to talk about what has happened. This can go so far that children place a veto on talking about the deceased person because it hurts so much. When this happens, we should be careful of pressuring them too much all at once, but, rather, look for occasions where it will be right to mention the dead person. Parents know their children well, and also know when it is opportune to start a conversation again:

Helen lost her little brother to sudden infant death syndrome (SIDS). Her parents said that for a period shortly following his death she would not talk about him, and she could not cry. Her father said: 'One day I went into her room and in a way forced her to talk about him. When I started to talk, this helped her to start talking. Before that, she always went to another room when we started to talk about him.'

Often, a child will signal to adults through play, drawings or in other ways, that they think about what has happened. These signals are unfortunately often overlooked by adults. We know from research that parents underestimate the consequences critical events have for children; how much children think of and are occupied by what has happened (see Weller *et al.* 1991; Yule and Williams 1990). Adults do not seem to want to see or understand this, and it is not accidental that adults often use the phrase 'out of sight, out of mind' to describe how children deal with traumatic events. Unfortunately, reality is different, and as adults we have to improve our ability to identify children's signals. This necessitates adequate counselling for carers responsible for children in grief. Such counselling will help them provide for children's needs.

Sometimes children cope by being preoccupied with the lost person. Photo albums and available video films are watched, other memories are reviewed and the grave is visited. Through looking at pictures and other things, the child can relive things they did together with the dead person. Smaller children may recreate an event to master it better:

> In a kindergarten where a child was killed in an accident, the remaining children's parents (in a parents' meeting) told how the children were playing the accidental event at home in the manner they thought the event had happened. In the kindergarten they had seen little of this play. Before this parents' meeting the personnel in the kindergarten had been unsure of how to deal with the event, and maybe the children had 'understood' that they should keep their play for home.

Adults must not only accept such play, but actively help children to work through their reactions through play. The play can help children to bring order and coherence to a chaos of thoughts. Through play, parts of the puzzle fall into place, and they can gradually regain security in their life. The following example shows how play is used as part of an active mastery of death:

> Seven-year-old Roger often went alone to his brother's grave site. It lay on his way to school. He made a small grave beside his brother's grave and in that he buried a homemade casket (matchbox) with a dead bee inside. He ordered his parents not to touch the grave, and after a few months he dug the casket up to see what had happened to the bee.

Many children carry out burial rites in sand or earth, where they bury dead animals or insects. In this way they try to understand the death process and get a better grip on what has happened. They may also make drawings of graves, crosses or an undertaker's car, or they may draw other events or things connected with the death. Such activities help their understanding of what has happened. Children master other difficult things in life in the same manner. An example is children's play following a hospital stay, when they play nurse or doctor and let a friend be the patient. In this way, they can represent and 'part with' their stressful experience. In the same way that many hospitals actively stimulate such play by providing appropriate toys, parents and other adults can help children to cope actively with a death by giving smaller children opportunities to play out or in other ways express their experiences and reactions.

Through play children can take traumatic experiences apart and put them together again, and they can do this at one step removed from reality. They can toss and turn over in their minds how things happened, and they can also reduce tension by imagining a happy ending to the event. Through play children may express feelings and thoughts that can be difficult to express directly.

If a parent or carer finds that the play has taken on a rigid, sad or repetitive character, they should talk openly with the child. They may have become lonely in their play. Repetitive play that does not seem to help the child in any way should be of concern to adults, and lead to the seeking of professional guidance.

Some parents have introduced dolls or fantasy figures to help children in grief. Both directly and indirectly children can use such figures to work through aspects of what is happening or has happened. The following example illustrates this:

> A father used a fantasy family that he had made up earlier together with his five-year-old son, Ken, when he had to explain to Ken the seriousness of the illness of Ken's mother. She had cancer, and it was obvious that she would not survive. The fantasy family 'lived' somewhere in the county, and consisted of a father, a mother and a son the same age as Ken. Ken's father made up a story that the fantasy boy went into the wood one day with his father to cut trees. When it was time for a break in their work, they sat down, and then the fantasy father told his boy that his mother was so sick that she might die. Ken at once understood the point, turned to his father and asked: 'Will you marry again?'

Maybe it was unnecessary of the father to use the fantasy family to tell the boy the news, but it gave him a way of doing this that he felt comfortable with.

To let children visit the grave is important for their grief. Such visits are not as emotionally laden as participation in seeing the dead body or being part of the funeral. Bringing children along means acknowledging their grief, as well as providing a good opportunity to talk about feelings and thoughts. Children's relationship to a grave can be less personal than adults' and therefore parents can be quite relaxed if children do not want to go and visit the grave. Children's grief and longing cannot be measured in how interested they are in visiting the gravesite, and apart from visiting on important memorial dates children should not receive any pressure to participate, and even on those dates we should carefully encourage more than pressure.

When children are brought along, they have to be prepared for the sadness and tears they may see in their parents. A three-year-old asked his mother at his sister's grave: 'How long are you going to stay here and cry?'

Stimulate emotional coping

Emotional coping can best take place through open communication within the family. If a family member dies suddenly, it is most important that the family talks *together* about what has happened. This is especially so if one or more of the family members was present when it happened, as they have important information needed by those not present to understand what happened. Unfortunately, children often receive only partial information about what has happened, and are often only given it little by little. Help from an outside person who stimulates talking with the whole family present is helpful after sudden, unexpected deaths:

> In a family where a father hung himself a son in his early teens came into the room right after his mother had managed to get him down on the floor. He helped with resuscitation but the father died later in the hospital. The mother said to her son that he had a heart failure, and it was only the following day that he haphazardly heard that this was a suicide. Without a conversation about the mother's attempt at secrecy and follow-up conversations that helped keeping the communication lines open in the family in the aftermath, full communication failure might have resulted.

It is not uncommon that family secrets are established after dramatic deaths, and important information is kept from children. Good follow-up from healthcare workers where the family meet role models who manage to speak openly about difficult issues and provide family members, including children, with an opportunity to talk about what has happened and the changed situation within the family, can be important help to ensure that the family copes well over time (Dyregrov 2001b).

With the increase in fear and anxiety following a death, it is best to try to secure as much continuity as possible both at home and at the play group or school. By keeping to known and dear routines, a secure shell is made within what is chaotic and frightening. Play group and school may become a firm foundation in an otherwise insecure situation, and we have found that it is helpful to keep absences to a minimum when there is a death in a family. This requires good communication between home and school, and the guidelines outlined in the following chapter should be followed.

At home, separations should be kept to a minimum. Some parents think it best to let children be with grandparents or good friends immediately following a death, as they feel they cannot give them enough attention. What they often are unaware of is how sensitive children, especially the younger ones, are to separations. Usually it is much better to let children stay with grieving parents, rather than to send them away. Being sent away can result in strong fear that their parents or remaining parent will disappear. There are, however, some situations where parents are so grief-stricken that they are unable to care adequately for their children. In such situations it is best that some close relative or friend comes to the home and helps, rather than moving the child or children out.

Children's need to be close to their parents, to sleep with their door open and so on, must be met. That children become more clinging following a death can be very demanding of parents, but most often the child's behaviour will normalize fairly soon if this need is met. Meeting this need in such situations does not mean letting the child take command, but means meeting the child's need for closeness and security. Letting a child sleep in the parents' bed for a while may be necessary, but the goal should be to re-establish normal routine quickly.

The fear children have of the potential death of their parents or themselves needs to be talked about. They need assurances that nothing will happen to them or their parents. They need information that it is usual for children to become afraid for their parents when somebody close to them dies. If one of the parents is dead, they need to know that, even if their remaining parent becomes ill, this does not mean that he or she will die also. It is most important to give words to the fear of repetition.

Children also need to have it explained why parents may become so anxious for them – so anxious that it has an impact on the way they are treated:

> Tom (15) became very irritated by his mother when she came to fetch him in front of his friends one evening when he was half an hour late coming home. His mother's fear that something might have happened to him overtook her, because his non-arrival triggered fantasies about things that could have happened. Four months earlier her other son was killed.

Parents and other carers ought also to talk to children about possible guilt feelings or self-reproach. It is usually best to choose a situation where it is natural to talk about the dead person, for example when the children themselves mention him or her. The primary message is: 'Sometimes it happens that children think that it is something they have done, thought or said that caused the death. Have you had any such thoughts?' If the answer is affirmative the subsequent conversation must aim to bring the child's thoughts forward. Whether the answer is yes or no it should be clearly conveyed to the child that 'nothing you have thought, said or done could have caused what happened'. What is said has to be tailored to the situation and the child's age, but the main thing is that self-reproach should be prevented.

Smaller children need reassurance that they will be taken care of. After a parent's death children may show anxiety concerning who will attend to their daily needs. If possible they need to know that they do not have to move, and that the family will have money (perhaps through insurance) for food and clothing. Smaller children may wonder who will make food for them, and should be told early on who will take care of them, to counteract this 'primary' anxiety.

Longing for the lost one can be quite severe at times. Adults must help the child to tolerate this, tell the child that even though the longing can be strong for a long time, eventually it will hurt a little less. Adults should tell them that it helps to talk about it, that looking at pictures, holding things that belonged to the lost person and visiting places they went together can ease the pain. Adults also have to let the child know that they do not have to react as the adults do – that they are free to react as they want to, and that nobody will demand that they have to be sad all the time.

As children grow and develop they will return to the loss more mature and with more understanding. They can reflect over the loss, seek information about the causes of the death and ascribe new meaning to their own acts or thoughts, as well as change the inner image they harbour of the lost person. How the child's parent or remaining parent is able to talk about the lost person over time is essential for how the child will handle the grief. In families with an open communication style where the child experiences a safe environment with room for their questions, thoughts and feelings, they can gradually develop new understanding of what happened with increasing age. Conversations about the death over time should include the child's own understanding and narrative alongside family members who help in filling this narrative. The co-construction of the story where family members jointly build the story of what happened seems conducive to children's understanding of and living with loss over time. A so-called 'elaborative' style allows for better coping over time than one where conversations are not allowed or one person has the hegemony or dominates the story (Bohanek *et al.* 2006; Harley and Reese 1999). Salmon and Bryant (2002) have pointed out the following important functions of talking about an important event with children:

- it helps them keep the event in memory and not forget it

- it helps the child assess and interpret what happened

- it corrects misunderstandings

- it helps the child to handle and regulate their emotions

- it provides information about coping strategies and promotes the use of these.

During childhood children depend upon their interplay with parents and other adults to learn to regulate emotions. An open communication style with conversations about difficult themes and feelings helps children to develop their capacity for emotional regulation, a learning they benefit from throughout life. From being dependent on an adult who consoles, calms down, puts words to feelings, touches and supports and so on, they can gradually learn how to soothe themselves when feelings become strong, and they internalize this capacity. In the interplay with parents they gradually develop expertise in understanding, foreseeing, monitoring and especially changing their feelings (Diamond and Aspinwall 2003). As a consequence of a parent becoming more inaccessible as a support person and because children's feelings can be so strong that they are not able to regulate them when a death (or divorce) happens in the family, there is a danger that the acquisition of emotional regulation suffers. In such situations the child may cope by shutting out or avoiding the memory and the feelings it evokes:

> Eva (14) lost her best friend in an accident when she was six years old. Her parents were divorced and Eva lived with her mother who had psychiatric problems. Eva said that she had only herself to rely on and that she did not talk with her mother or anyone else. Some years later her father died and she again used what she had become good at, making herself become 'hard', suppressing her emotions. Two other deaths in her social vicinity were handled in the same way, and when she was sent to a psychologist because of her school problems, she presented herself as someone who had learnt that there was no one else there for her. 'I am an expert in pushing all feelings away, regardless of them being good or bad,' she said.

Having actively to suppress our emotions is regarded as negative for both our health and social life (John and Gross 2004; Pennebaker 1997). In the aftermath of violent death caregivers can exert pressure on the child to refrain from communicating or to 'forget' what happened, as well as meeting the child's questions with evasion (Kaplow et al. 2006), as the caregivers struggle to make sense and cope with what has happened. Elaboration or co-construction becomes difficult in such a climate.

Conversations with parents or the remaining parent where children perceive the presence of parents who are able to be there with care, support and warmth in their weak days following a death can be invaluable when they are to regulate difficult thoughts and strong feelings. With understanding and empathic parents the children can learn to downregulate feelings when they become too strong and let them in when they shut them out too much. Both over-regulation and under-regulation of feelings can be negative for children, and good interplay with parents makes for flexible coping mechanisms that help them manage both the present and possible future difficult situations.

Over time children, especially when they reach school age, can be helped to get a better grip on their feelings and thoughts by asking them questions such as:

- If you could speak to _____ (name of the deceased) about what has happened to you after his/her death, what would you have said?

- If you could have said something to _____ before the death, what would you have said?

- If you could have asked him/her about anything what would it have been?

- How do you think that _____ has influenced you as a person?

- What do you think he/she would have told you if there had been time for it before his/her death?

By asking them to write the answers down, the task concretizes and structures children's inner thoughts and feelings.

Chapter Eight

Handling death in the play group and at school

———————

Being prepared before a death occurs

All schools have to deal with deaths. It is a clear advantage in such situations if the school is prepared to deal with such events. Experience has shown that *mental preparation and planning* before a death or other critical event occurs leads to a much better handling than if we 'take things as they come'. It is helpful to instigate new measures that increase the school's preparedness.

- Let handling of death in the school or classroom setting be the theme for a teachers' meeting.

- Organize or send teachers and/or other staff members (all or specially selected) to a course on children and death.

- Select a smaller group of teachers or preschool teachers to increase their knowledge in this area, so that they can be a resource group for the other staff.

- Make sure that the school or kindergarten has relevant literature that can be used by interested staff, and material/literature and web addresses that can be used in the classroom or play group.

- Formulate, have easily available and regularly update plans for how the school or kindergarten will deal with different smaller or larger serious crisis situations that potentially may happen or affect the institution. Specify who will do what, and make a list of resource people who may be called upon in such situations. Consider designating a telephone line to be used in such emergencies. Secure good contact with mental health agencies and designate who you will use as consultants ahead of an event, as the school can be invaded by all kinds of helpers in a larger event. Let the contingency plan be available on the school's web page for parents and others to know about it.

- Have plans of action ready for the situations that are most likely to happen to 'your' school, that is, based on an evaluation of what kind of event (i.e. type of natural or man-made disaster) that can be expected to have an impact on your area.

- In response to an event, quickly establish the involved people, what has happened, how it happened and what information has been given out. On the basis of this information, the necessary action can be taken.

Even though most of what is written in this book can be used in dealing with larger events that can hit a school, the amount of work that has to be instigated in a larger accident is only touched upon. This is not the main focus of this book, and interested readers are referred to Klingman (1987), La Greca et al. (2002), Nader and Pynoos (1993), Saylor (1993),

Toubiana *et al.* (1988) and Yule and Gold (1993) for information on children's responses to such events and how to organize work within the school in such events.

Teachers as a resource group

Teachers (both play group- and schoolteachers) are important in caring for children when a death affects a school. Teachers are a resource group for several reasons:

- Teachers know the individual child and their personality.

- Teachers know the 'culture' within each class.

- Teachers are experts in providing children with knowledge, more so than psychologists and psychiatrists.

- Teachers have knowledge about involvement pedagogics, and know how to help children use a variety of expressive means to deal with critical events.

- Teachers are well known and trusted by the children.

These aspects make teachers a unique resource for dealing with children's needs when a death occurs that has an impact on the school.

Teachers' own needs

When a death has an impact on a play group or school, this will also affect the teachers to some extent. Some teachers are so affected that they are not able to care for their pupils or students properly because they themselves have such strong reactions:

One of the teachers of a nursery school was killed in a tragic accident. The way the accident happened, together with the close relationship between the staff, led to very strong reactions among the colleagues. In a meeting for the staff they were helped to put words to their impressions and reactions. Among other reactions, they talked about their sadness, the unreality of the situation, their anxiety and uncertainty about how to inform the children, and how to handle the situation. In this case, the staff had difficulty taking care of the children's needs before they themselves had a better grip of the situation. The format of a meeting to take care of the needs of the staff is similar to that described for a class-room-meeting later, and based on Jeffrey T. Mitchell's *Critical Incident Stress Debriefing* format (Mitchell 1983) that I have described as psychological debriefing in more detail elsewhere (Dyregrov 2002).

Teachers' fear of not being able to take care of the children is similar to that experienced by many parents. In some situations teachers have to put their own needs aside, 'pull themselves together' and do the job of confronting their class before they themselves have had an opportunity to talk about what has happened. Teachers can do this; they have done so before, and it is important that they carry out such tasks. But they also have to address their own needs, either by talking with a reliable colleague or by gathering as a group for a thorough talk-through of their impressions and reactions.

Sometimes teachers refrain from their task of talking to their students about what has happened because they think this is too difficult for them, or they feel that it is too much responsibility for themselves. It is hoped that this book will help to provide the knowledge that will increase teachers' and others' ability to deal with such situations.

Sometimes teachers want a psychologist or other mental health professional to talk to the children, and sometimes mental health professionals themselves want to meet the children face to face. In my opinion this should not be the norm as it undermines the position of the teachers, and because if this happens the students have to talk to a stranger in whom they first have to build trust. Mental health professionals should counsel the teachers on how they can deal with the situation, or be a support that interacts with the teacher in the classroom. However, some situations are so grave that a psychologist or other professional can be used in direct contact with the students:

> In an upper secondary school three students in the same class took their life within a year. The seriousness of the situation led the school management to invite a psychologist to be with school personnel when the class was gathered to talk through what had happened after the second suicide. This suicide took place right before the summer holiday and before measures were implemented at the start of the new school year, the third student took his life. He was the only person not present at the meeting after the second suicide. An individual assessment of all students led to follow-up measures for those identified at risk, alongside other measures undertaken to support the school management.

How the situation is dealt with in the school will depend on who is dead and how the death happened. Some deaths, for example the death of a teacher or student, will have an impact on the whole school, whereas others, for example a parent's death, will have an impact on a class or on some students. If an accident occurs on the way to or from the school, or during an excursion, or a child has committed suicide, this will be different from a death from a long-lasting disease. If several students are killed in the same accident, this will have serious consequences for the school's ordinary life.

Terminal illness of a child

Although this book focuses primarily on sudden death, some comments on handling a terminal illness in the classroom will be included.

When a child has a serious and possibly life-threatening disease, the family (including the child, of course) and the school should delineate what the class should be told about absences, exclusion from sports or other activities, and return following treatments that may result in changes of appearance or ability to participate fully in class. It is advisable that although physical limitations require some special treatment, behavioural standards should be maintained, as should as much of the school routine as possible. Homebound teaching may be needed at times, especially towards the final stage of life.

Being able to maintain school routines can be especially important for seriously ill children. It mobilizes hope, encourages social contact and reinforces the living child within them. Seriously ill and dying children often cope best with their condition by living as fully as they can until they die. During serious illness, the school may represent one of the few areas where the child feels a sense of control and accomplishment.

Including the child in the class situation throughout the course of the illness also helps the class to deal with the situation. Opportunities for art activity and creative expression can help the class in working through both the cognitive and emotional ramifications of a classmate's serious disease. Communication between the hospital staff, the parents and school personnel is important for the integration of a sick child in the school community.

By having hospital personnel or other knowledgeable adults present to inform and discuss the disease with the class, the children can better understand their sick classmate, and their fear of getting the same disease can be reduced. The sick child is often an 'expert' on his or her own disease, knowing the right terminology and how the disease and treatment works in the body.

When the child becomes unable to attend school, it can be very supportive to let classmates visit the child at home or in the hospital. This must be worked out in close contact with the family, as some sick children find such visits too exhausting. Visits by the teacher may be much welcomed by both child and parents. Some children, especially adolescents, have a great longing for contact with their friends and schoolmates in this phase, and may feel very rejected or let down if no one comes to visit. The teacher can play an important role in channelling visits at this stage of the disease:

> A 15-year-old boy dying of a brain tumour wrote three versions of this letter to his class, a letter that was never sent: 'Hello. Long time no see. There is still life in me (barely). I have a new bed that can be regulated. In this I sit day in and day out, and it is very boring. It is hard to talk, stand or use my fingers. I am shivering and need a computer keyboard to be able to write. I VERY MUCH WANT TO BECOME WELL AGAIN. Otherwise my time passes in reading and sleeping. There is still some hope, but not much. It is more fun to be well, and to attend school. I think a lot about you and hope to be able to come to class soon. Otherwise, there is nothing more to tell you, I hope all will be well...
> PS. If you are not too busy, I would appreciate a visit.

Children miss their schoolfriends, and contact should be retained if possible. The child also worries about how peers and teachers react to their illness, and a visit from the teacher, where this is discussed, can alleviate unnecessary distress in the child.

The need of individual students

Students who have experienced a death in the close family will usually do best if they go back to school as soon as possible. The first school day following an absence in relation to a death can be difficult. The transition can be made easier by early contact between the teacher and the home. When a teacher initiates this contact, it shows that he or she cares and will try to help as much as possible. It is beneficial if the student can plan for his or her meeting with the class together with the teacher. It is helpful for the child if the teacher that the student most trusts participates in this preparation.

Even though the teacher is responsible for his or her class, it may be a good thing if the student can be included in the decision of what will be said in the class. This gives the student a sense of control. Sometimes, but not often, a student wants to give the information him- or herself. Most often they want the teacher to tell the class, either before they arrive themselves or while they are present.

It is helpful if the other students are told how the bereaved student wants them to behave towards him or her. Even though it is best that a death is openly and naturally talked about, some students do not want others to talk about what has happened – and it is important to respect their need. Usually bereaved students understand that their fellow students need information, especially when they are told why this is so, to prevent rumours, counteract anxiety and so forth. Even though the student may not want the death talked about, some deaths (suicide, murder) may affect many students because of their dramatic quality. In such cases the teacher must explain to the student in question why it is necessary to talk about this with the other students.

That parents and teachers underestimate children's difficulties after traumatic events has already been mentioned. At school, children in grief can experience great difficulty in concentrating, without teachers being aware of how this is linked to the loss. In a small Norwegian study of 32 adolescents who were bereaved by suicide attending upper secondary school, more than half experienced serious post-traumatic problems (Dyregrov 2006). They reported lower grades and increased absence from school. As many as 43% marked on a questionnaire that they 'almost always' had problems concentrating and the rest experienced this to some degree. Taking over adult tasks from parents who were unable to sustain such tasks may explain some of these results. Regardless of the increased pressure, they are expected to keep up their school performance and results.

In this small study (Dyregrov 2006) it also became apparent that many of the adolescents felt that they were not believed when they said that they were struggling and that the loss made it difficult to keep up with schoolwork. Following situations where they were able to keep memories at bay to take part in pleasurable activities, the students especially felt that teachers were suspicious of them trying to shirk their duty. When they tried to do their best regardless of concentration difficulties or headaches, they developed depressive thoughts when they always felt themselves under pressure and had difficulties keeping up their performance from before the death:

> On the preliminaries this year I had a constant headache and really could not concentrate. I told them but they did not listen. You do your best and have big problems concentrating and get a low grade. Then the teacher comments that: 'you should have done better, I know you can.' That is really depressing. (Boy, 14)

Teachers may even give the students extra homework or corrections which further add to their problems and increase the feeling of not being understood. This does not necessarily happen immediately after the loss, but often after some time has elapsed, when the relation between the difficulties in concentration and the death is not so obvious. As soon as teachers are made aware of this connection, they can show great understanding for students' needs. Many grieving students complain of teachers' short memory. Even though they may be met with much understanding when they return to school, they experience that their loss is soon forgotten:

> Some months following a brother's death an adolescent girl experienced that one of her teachers asked: 'Anyone here who has lost a loved one lately?' This girl really struggled to find firm ground under her feet following her brother's death and with the experience that the teachers did not understand, this remark was only a token of how little they cared or understood. A meeting was held with all teachers at her school present. She met them together with her psychologist. Here they first heard a short presentation of usual reactions and problems that adolescents experience following a loss with a focus on school problems, before the teachers could ask the student questions. After this she experienced that her situation at school improved. Her best friend was also allowed to attend this meeting as a support for her.

Even in the kindergarten some children complain about the adults' short memory. A boy formulated it in this way:

> 'Everyone has forgotten about my dad. We do not talk about my dad in the kindergarten.'

Schools need to know and acknowledge that even children who witness serious accidents and disasters may suffer from severe after-effects. This is known from major disasters, such as the fire at the Bradford football stadium in England, when many children witnessed people burning to death. Teachers in neighbouring schools refused to acknowledge that children could suffer after-effects from this fire (Yule and Williams 1990). From my own clinical experience it is clear that bystanders and witnesses form a group of 'hidden' victims, with reactions that often go unrecognized by the adult world.

Some students will fall behind in their schoolwork. It is necessary that at intervals teachers assess the need for special sessions at school. Most children can do without this, but some develop serious concentration problems, especially when the death happened in dramatic circumstances. Students with such problems need extra educational resources. It is easy for teachers to underestimate the duration of the student's problems. Several reports have shown that children who experience trauma and loss can have their learning capacity reduced, have more absence from school, evidence lower performance and so on (see Dyregrov 2004 for an overview). There is a clear relationship between the school's handling of a crisis situation and the student's report of post-traumatic complaints (Broberg, Dyregrov and Lilled 2005).

For students who struggle over time it may be important to arrange for educational support in addition to adjusting the amount of homework. Feedback on tests can be adjusted and extra time at exams may be added. To increase concentration and memory the students may need to learn relaxation techniques, be taught techniques that can reduce intrusive material, receive more support, encouragement and feedback on good performance than other students and gradually have the expectations for school performance increased. The following measures based on Dyregrov (2006) can make grieving children's learning environment optimal:

- Do not attract attention to the student without him or her being prepared.

- Care and sympathy should be adjusted to the student's wishes, but it should be kept in mind that reactions have a long-term perspective.

- A plan for educational assistance and psychological support at school should be made for the grieving child.

- Strategies must be synchronized between different teachers in order for the child to experience consistency in their teacher's care and behaviour.

- The student must be allowed 'time out' if something becomes difficult, or even having reduced days in periods. Let the student know where they can go for support if they leave a session (school nurse, contact teacher, office and so on). Let a good friend leave the classroom with them if necessary. Contact the student after the session.

- Adjust tasks in a way that increases the chance of the students managing them (assisted learning).

- Feedback must be based on the student's temporary learning capacity, not on previous level of function. By adjusting the pressure on grades and providing much positive feedback for what the student is able to achieve, motivation and pleasure in school work is kept as much as possible.

- Accept that the student can be more passive at school for a period without this affecting his or her grades.

- Extra time at tests or dropping tests must be initiated if needed.

- The student can be given extra assistance in subjects that are especially problematic.

Good contact between home and school with counselling of the parents regarding pressure in relation to homework and information about how a loss can influence school performance will also be appropriate.

How to give notification of a death at school

Sometimes the difficult task of notifying a child about a close family member's death has to be done by a teacher. With modern technology text messages can make it almost impossible to wait with death notification:

> A 20-year-old man was killed in a car crash. The parents were notified by their daughter who was called by a friend who had witnessed the crash. Parents wanted to wait until they could get to their other son (15) to tell him personally about what had happened. They were not able to reach him until an hour had elapsed. When they told him he said that he had known about this from right after the crash as one of his friends had attended the scene soon after it happened and had sent a text message.

Although it would be best to have someone from the child's closest family come to a school to notify the child, this task may have to be carried out by a representative for the school. Schematically, the following can be added:

- The person that gives the notification should be somebody the student trusts, preferably the primary teacher.

- Before the child is told, make sure that the necessary information concerning when and how the death happened is available.

- The teacher should select a suitable place, free from disturbance.

- The news should be given openly, truthfully and directly, but with some time for mental preparation (see Chapter Seven). The person conveying the message should get down on the child's level. Whom the message concerns should be stated immediately to prevent time to speculate who the information is about. The notification should not be delayed to the end of the school day, and information about the seriousness of the situation should not be delayed until they come home. If several siblings attend the same school they should be informed together.

- Time must be set aside to sit with the student after the news has been broken, so that slower reactions can be allowed expression. One should secure that the information is understood. If the child has just reached school age what it means to be dead could be shortly explained.

- The teacher should refrain from using phrases such as: 'Everything will turn out right', 'Time heals all wounds' and so forth. For the youngest school children one can say: 'Remember that nothing you have done or thought caused the death to happen.'

- Don't let the student be alone; comfort him or her in a natural way. Physical contact can have a comforting effect, but if the student does not want this, this should be respected. Do not put phrases in the child's mouth or try to stimulate an emotional reaction because you think it is important. The shock may lead many children to appear relatively unaffected without this being a strange reaction.

- The teacher should accompany the student home or to where the rest of the family is staying.

- With the student's or family's permission, the rest of the class should be told as soon as possible.

Death notification is a difficult task, but teachers are able to do this, especially if they have prepared for such a task beforehand. If it is a larger event that affects many students (such as a community disaster), the principal should inform the whole school. He or she may ask the students to go to their classroom, where they will receive information. The teachers can then go to the classrooms and tell the students in a calm and direct manner.

Follow-up after such situations should follow the model for classroom meetings that is described later. In planning for memorials, older students can beneficially be involved.

Immediate intervention

In the immediate aftermath of a death that directly affects the school (a student's or teacher's death) emphasis should be placed on the following:

- lower distress (arousal), reduce uncertainty and create safety

- small children are reassured about adult presence and protection. Early reunion with parents is important if something happened in the kindergarten

- correct information about facts is spread to children, the home and others

- children are helped in getting a 'grip' on the situation; establish a time line on what happened

- build on the cohesion in the class or group

140 — GRIEF IN CHILDREN

- adults provide support

- shield or protect against unnecessary stress (media, onlookers)

- if a student or students died outside of school hours, the school can be opened for classmates and friends

- following a death, ritual commemorations are chosen, such as lighting candles, raising the flag at half-mast (see next paragraph).

With a plan for crisis situations the educational staff and other staff can appear calm and with authority that instigates trust in children and their caretakers (cf. crisis leadership later). The bodily distress and activation that is triggered by the situation will be moderated by the mobilization of support around the children, including bodily contact. In the immediate aftermath of a bigger event both children and adults will be occupied by accessing information: What has happened and with whom? Is someone they love involved? What happens now? Where can we learn more? The questions are many, the anxiety high, and gathering, spreading and updating information takes priority. Adequate handling of information represents good caring. To have systems in place that can make this happen is a very important part of crisis preparedness. That means that both technical and tactical resources (manning switchboards, handling incoming and outgoing calls, and media contacts) must be in place and function according to plan.

Rituals in the school: the funeral

When the death of a student or a teacher occurs, this has to be commemorated in the school or kindergarten. This can be done in several ways. A *memorial* service where all the students are gathered in the assembly hall allows for a dignified acknowledgement of what has happened, and provides the children with a meaningful way to express their grief and confront the reality of the loss. The content of a memorial service can be decided by the teachers, the administration of the school, the clergy and the students themselves. Sometimes such a memorial is planned at short notice, and it is best if the teachers have a plan for such a memorial worked out in advance. A memorial can include:

- memorial words by the school's principal
- memorial words by the class's primary teacher
- reading of a suitable poem by a student or teacher
- a short sermon or some words by a priest
- a song or musical piece; choosing the dead child's favourite song can be advisable.

The memorial site can be decorated with the children's art work and candles can be lit. The child's parents and siblings can be invited, as can close friends attending other schools. If the notification of a student's or teacher's death comes during the school day, some way of marking the death together may be found. Symbolic acts make it possible to express feelings directly, without having to use words. After a memorial the students can go to their classroom and take time to talk about what has happened. Depending on the type of event, either one class or the whole school will participate in the funeral. At the funeral they can symbolically express their grief by such acts as each child placing a flower, drawing or some other symbolic thing on the casket, or by having a representative from the class say some words, or place a wreath on the casket on behalf of the class.

Some deaths lead to a gathering of many people at the funeral. This is especially so with events that attract media interest, or when more than one person is to be buried at the same time. In such situations it can be helpful to let the students bid farewell collectively, in a ceremony separate from the funeral:

> In a situation where a teacher was killed, the school administration, together with representatives of the church, decided that the students could come to the chapel one hour before the funeral took place. There they could bid farewell to their teacher, and they could individually go to the casket with a flower, and at the same time place a wreath from the class on the casket. If the students had waited with their commemoration until the funeral, it would have been lost among all the people who came to the funeral. The students were free to be present during the funeral as well, if they so wanted.

At funerals involving a lot of media interest, teachers and adults should know that students easily feel invaded by journalists and photographers who want to present their grief to the public. Let me include some comments made by adolescents after such an event:

> 'All the photographers and the journalists should have been banned from the event. When they take close-ups of us and almost jump on us, it is hard to show feelings the way you want to.'

> 'I cried a little inside the church, but the hardest part was to walk out where all the press people were ready. Almost all the girls were crying when we went out of church. I almost felt that I was not part of the funeral. I felt it was all unreal. It was sad, especially with all the photographers that left nobody any peace.'

> 'I felt that everything was extremely sad and incomprehensible. But I just could not cry, only sat in silence. I do not think

that the press people should have been allowed there. They ruined everything.'

It is important that teachers and other adults shield the students from press representatives who prevent them from expressing their grief, or who exploit their grief. Representatives of the police, church and school should work out an agreement with the press that ensures respect for the children in such a way that pictures and interviews are only allowed with the consent of students and parents.

Although it is important that children who have lost siblings, parents or grandparents can take part in the viewing of the dead, we should be careful of including all children in a class or group in such rituals if a fellow student dies. A viewing may be emotionally intense and sensory impressions can be etched into memory and lead to intrusive recollections afterwards. In a study among Finnish secondary school students, it was found that participation in the viewing following a student's death was associated with more trauma reactions and more intense grief (Poijula *et al.* 2001b). Adults must make a sound assessment of whom should participate in such a ritual. There is a short distance between what is helpful and what will be an extra burden in relation to viewing a dead body. When a student has a close relationship to the deceased, has been a best friend, participation should be allowed, otherwise a student should not be routinely included. If many students are to participate what has already been written about preparation for and care in the situation should be emphasized.

Classroom memorial and other rituals

There are several ways of commemorating a death in the classroom. It is important to let the children be involved in choosing how this is done. The meaningful use of rituals facilitates emotional expression and intellectual understanding, and is very much in tune with children's developmental needs.

If a student dies, his or her immediate class group can be the centre of a symbolic expression that he or she is dead. The students can do drawings which can decorate their shared space, or they can create one joint drawing, knit a carpet or make some other thing that can be placed on the table.

Candles have always had a strong symbolic value for human beings, and they can be used to commemorate a dead student. Having a photograph and lighting a candle and letting it burn during the days until his or her funeral marks the absence in a fine way.

Students can do other things together: they can plant a tree; make something for the bereaved parents; engage in accident prevention activities and so forth. The possibilities are numerous and the students themselves usually come up with many ideas and thoughts about what can be done. The teacher's task is to channel the creativity in ways that help the children to give concrete expression to their grief. This is important at all age levels, because symbolic events give direct expression to inner thoughts and feelings.

Symbolic acts also help students to give form and structure to 'chaotic' thoughts and feelings. By letting thoughts and feelings become acts, children can make the 'incomprehensible' concrete. Children, as do adults, often feel better after taking part in symbolic acts.

Children, and especially adolescents, use ritual expression in relation to a death of a friend. Such spontaneous rituals can include gathering at the site of the death to commemorate their grief by putting flowers, poems, objects they associate with the deceased and so on, at the scene. They may seek out this place for days and find comfort in being where their friend died. Gradually, the custom of roadside memorials is spreading, allowing for emotional expression. As adults we should respect the need for such commemorations and even help in securing a site for their use, but at the same time we may gently need to advise when to step down this activity as that sometimes seems difficult to do. Spontaneous rituals can be very personal since no one has special rights or precedence at them, in contrast with more public rituals such as the memorial at school or the burial. The personal expression of a friend's importance, which such spontaneous rituals allow for, appears to fill deep emotional as well as social needs. It is as if the presence of the deceased is directly tied to the place where he or she died in such a way that it obtains a special psychological value for different expressions of grief and longing. In many ways this place is, for a period of time, more important for young people than the grave.

Adolescents increasingly use the internet to express their grief, communicate and show their compassion with the family and commemorate their loss. They make web pages in memory of their dead friend with pictures and a description of the person. Here, both those who knew the deceased, and others can formulate their thoughts and reactions about what has happened. By communicating with those responsible for such web pages in Norway I have learnt that they often are constructed and maintained by boys, while both genders actively write their expressions. Parents of the deceased sometimes use such pages to communicate with the group of friends, for example about how much they would like visits to the home. While such web pages obviously serve important needs for adolescents, as adults we should be conscious that it can be a major responsibility to maintain them, especially as the time since death increases. The adolescents responsible for this may need some gentle advice and support in stepping down this activity without thinking that this is devaluing the person they lost. Parents often find comfort in looking at such pages as they relay the role their son or daughter still plays in other people's minds, and they keep the memory alive. This also means that parents sometimes want to take over the responsibility of maintaining web pages.

Classroom meeting about the death

Earlier in this book individual reactions to grief in children were described. But the effects of a death which affects a whole class or school will often be seen at the group level as well. Teachers may face more discipline problems in class or in the playground, with the children being more restless, talkative and disobedient. Teachers also have to deal with the spreading of rumours and misleading information, and children may exhibit inattention, lack of energy and motivational difficulties.

A helpful measure to counteract such effects is to follow a structured format in talking about the death in the classroom. This format can also be used in other settings, and may be used in class after critical events other than deaths. Such conversations can be used for groups of children or adolescents who were especially affected by the death, such as those who witnessed the death.

There are several positive aspects with such groups. Children and adolescents:

- have a chance to set words to different aspects of their experience
- have a chance to hear viewpoints from others in the same situation
- can express feelings in a safe context
- can activate the support of friends
- have a chance to help others by relating facts, providing support or listening

- have new and alternative perspectives

- learn how others cope with the situation and get ideas of what they can do themselves

- get information about usual reactions to such an event, and get their reactions acknowledged by others

- can receive specific advice on how they can cope with bothersome after-effects such as intrusive recollections, sleep disturbances and so forth

- can be identified for further help if necessary.

About two hours should be set aside for this meeting. The meeting should not be interrupted by breaks, although sometimes this is necessary with younger children. For smaller children it may also take less time. It is best if two teachers conduct the meeting together, as it can be demanding to bear the responsibility alone. The accompanying teacher should be known to the class beforehand. If the school has established a resource group for crisis situations, it is better if a member of this group can participate together with the primary teacher of the class.

The structure of the meeting should be as follows:

- introduction

- facts

- thoughts

- reactions

- information

- end.

Introduction

During the introduction phase the teacher explains what will take place in the coming hours, and why. It is emphasized that when someone dies, this often leaves many impressions and reactions that it is important to talk about and to set apart time for, because this helps us to get a better grip on what has happened. When somebody dies, we are filled with thoughts and feelings that make us sad, and we may become frightened or angry. Through talking about the event, we are better able to understand how others react, and misunderstandings can be prevented. It can be helpful to tell the students that it may 'hurt' to talk about the death, but that talking about it in the classroom may make it hurt less over time.

The leader of the conversation should also set some rules that should be followed.

- They are not to tell children outside of class what their classmates have experienced, thought or felt. They may retell what they said themselves or what they thought, but are not to retell what others have experienced. Even though it is not certain that this rule will be followed, it teaches the children to respect others.

- Nobody should be criticized afterwards for what they have said or how they reacted. If somebody cries or gets angry it is all right, and they should not be teased afterwards.

- Each child is to talk for him or herself, and not for others.

- They do not *have* to talk in the classroom, apart from telling how they learned about what happened. If they prefer, they may sit and listen for the rest of the meeting.

Facts

In the fact phase the students say how they learned about what happened, what they heard or were told, and how (where, when and by whom). This helps to put the event together from beginning to end, and to draw out relevant information from children who know a lot for the benefit of children who only know a little of what has happened. But, above all, it provides an opportunity to learn about and correct misunderstandings and confusion, and gives the class a common platform from which to understand the event.

Through this examination of facts the teacher will also find out whether some children are more directly affected by the event than others. These may be children that witnessed the death, or who learned about it in a 'brutal' way. In relation to what was written earlier concerning intrusive, strong memories, this information is particularly important in understanding after-effects and in providing adequate help for those students who need it.

The teacher may add the information that he or she has. Before the meeting, the teacher should get as much relevant information as possible about the chain of events and what is known about the cause of death, and relate this information to the children. After some events it may be useful to invite police officers or others to the class to give the students direct information about the events:

> In the immediate follow-up of a group of adolescents who were present at a party where an adolescent killed himself in front of many of them, it became clear that many of the young people showed deep anger towards ambulance personnel who came to the house. They blamed them for coming so late and for not doing enough to save their friend's life. We thought it best to have the ambulance personnel present at the debriefing meeting, which was held

one and a half days after the death. Here the adolescents could learn why the ambulance personnel handled the situation as they did, as well as learning the real time that had elapsed before the ambulance arrived. The ambulance personnel were able to show that the ambulance had in fact arrived at the scene very quickly after the event. In such situations the time sense changes, and minutes can feel like an eternity. We were able to provide the students with information that explained this for them. The ambulance personnel also had other relevant information that contributed to the adolescents getting a better grip on what had happened. The anger that they felt toward the ambulance workers soon disappeared.

The need for concrete information is great in children, and often underestimated by adults. Events where a classroom meeting is necessary are often surrounded by many rumours and much anxiety. Anxiety can spread like waves on the water among children:

> On the day of a suicide in a ninth grade the rumour spread that this was a murder. The parents were informed about the need for informing the other students about the facts quickly and the following day teachers started the school day by providing the same information in all classes, namely that the police, based on the findings at the scene, was sure this was a suicide not a murder. The classmates of the victim received extra follow-up by a classroom conversation.

With anxiety sometimes running high after traumatic events, it is very important early on to address rumours and misconceptions that may lead to unnecessary problems among children. If an event has been covered in the press, paper clippings can be used for classroom discussion. This is also important because it provides access to discrepancies between what the children have heard or experienced and how the event is described in the press.

Thoughts

The question of what thoughts the children had when they learned about the event automatically leads to answers that reveal their reactions and impressions. If a group was involved in the critical event, it is important to have the children see how they were able to think in constructive ways. Usually they have made good decisions, reacted quickly and mobilized their mental resources. By focusing on what they did well or their good decision-making, coping is stimulated. Usually there is a sliding transition from the thought phase to the reaction phase.

Reactions

We should refrain from questions such as 'What did you feel when you learned about what happened?' as such a direct approach to feelings tends to impede feelings more than to foster them. The question: 'What made the strongest impression on you about what happened?', on the other hand, often stimulates the expression of reactions and impressions, and at the same time shows respect for what the child thinks is important.

When children witness a death, it is helpful for these children to put words to their impressions in a detailed way. These can be impressions in all sensory channels: sensory, auditory, tactile and olfactory. A detailed review can help to relieve the intensity of such impressions. If children do not mention such impressions, they can be asked directly: 'Did anybody hear him scream after he was hit by the bus?' Children who were not exposed to such strong impressions should not be exposed to the stories of those who were. If the whole class was present and took in the impressions, it will be natural to talk about this with all students together. If some of the class members were exposed to the same situation and experienced strong sensory impressions, they can talk through this together. If somebody has experienced especially gruesome impressions, he or she may need individual follow-up.

When children give words to impressions and reactions, the teacher should refrain from saying 'Yes that is normal', but instead ask: 'Did anybody else experience this in a similar way?' This helps children to see that they have similar reactions, and their thoughts and reactions are acknowledged and normalized.

It is during the reaction phase that children will tell of the many reactions and thoughts they have had after they learned what happened. They can be prompted to talk about how they reacted initially, later the same day, how the first night was, and how they feel now. Grief, longing, helplessness, fear and other reactions may come to the fore during this part of the session. The children are stimulated to share their reactions, whether they be dreams, anxiety or thoughts about the loss of impulse control (e.g. it is easy to think: 'What if my father got that angry, and shot us like Stephen's father did?') or reactions to reminders that trigger intrusive memories and fear.

In the youngest grades, the use of drawings and other expressions can be used in this phase. This can be introduced by saying: 'I will give each of you a sheet of paper on which you can express the thoughts or impressions you may have. You can choose what you want to draw.' If a death is caused by an accident or a violent act, we should be prepared for drawings that may show this in all its gruesomeness, with dismembered body parts or a condensation of the traumatic event. Often the drawings reflect the children's anger over what happened, and their fear of losing control of their feelings. But drawings may also show wish-fulfilment or undoing of the event, or be without any reference to what has happened.

It should be suggested that children not only be asked to draw something in relation to the death or event, but also a drawing where they depict what can be done to repair the damage, or how it is possible to work to prevent such events from occurring. Depending on the cause of death, a 'coping drawing' should be used, one where the child is given the opportunity to gain control or mastery of a traumatic situation.

If the teachers feel comfortable with it, they can ask the children to look at the empty desk of the dead student and have them think about the things they never got to say to him or her when he or she was alive. They can say this inside their heads, or they can say it aloud. They can end this by saying goodbye. This can be done in the following manner: 'Look at Roger's desk and tell him everything you think he should know, and then say goodbye to him.' Of course the children can write or draw their farewell in addition. If a child has committed suicide this can be a very helpful approach to help the children give words to the helplessness they feel, and to counteract any feelings of self-reproach or guilt they may harbour. On finishing this task, children could display their drawings. Children could also be stimulated to read stories and poems in honour of their dead classmate.

Children could be stimulated to write down (e.g. in diaries) their thoughts and reactions, or, as a task, to complete sentences such as:

'The first thing I heard about the event was...'

'The worst thing about what happened for me was...'

'The strongest impression for me was...'

'I feel sad when I think about...'

If it is a teacher who is dead, this may also be a good time to ask the children how they feel about another teacher taking the place of the dead teacher. Students may make comments such as: 'You are not my teacher', or they may react with resentment towards the replacement teacher. It is important that the new teacher acknowledges the value and love the students have felt for their teacher, declaring that he or she will never be able to be, nor does he or she aspire to be, that person, and also finds it natural that for some of them it will take some time before they are able to relate to him or her as their teacher.

It is the thought and reaction phases that take up most of the time. It is during these phases that the children get to talk about what has happened. The children may show strong emotional reactions, and if this happens, it is important that the teachers mobilize caring and support from the other children, and do not necessarily give it themselves. By letting a fellow student put an arm around a fellow student, or by asking how the others feel when Rosalyn is crying, cohesion and group support is strengthened. Children can be very caring, kind and supportive of each other, and it is the teachers' task to stimulate this. Children's prosocial behaviour (empathy) can indeed be stimulated in crisis situations.

It is important to emphasize that it is not a goal to provoke strong reactions in a group; the important goal is to let them hear that others can have similar thoughts and reactions to themselves. Strong emotional reactions are contagious and it requires calm and confident adult behaviour to counteract this.

Information

In the information phase, the teacher summarizes what the children have said, and pinpoints the similarities in their thoughts and reactions, thus normaliszing their experience. If one of the teachers has information about other children's reactions in similar situations, it may be appropriate to say something about this to normalize reactions further. In addition to this, information should be given about the normal reactions that can be expected following such events, for example the reactions described in Chapter One. Reactions such as fear and anxiety, anger, thoughts about revenge, guilt, self-reproach and sadness need to be mentioned, as well as the possibility that the event can interfere with concentration and memory in the time following the event. It is helpful for the children to know that they, to a lesser or greater extent, may continue to think about a tragic death for the weeks and months after the event. But they also need to be told that they do not have to experience such reactions to be normal. Following violent deaths the children need to be reassured about their own safety.

It can be helpful to give children (especially adolescents) a short and simple written summary with information about normal reactions to death or trauma. Such leaflets should be taken home for parents to read. Links to web pages with such folders can be found in the 'Internet resources' at the end of this book.

During the information phase the teacher may give advice on what the students can do to get a better grip on what happened. This can include advice such as:

- talk with parents about the event
- talk with friends about the event
- visit the grave
- get more information about what happened
- write poems, diaries, letters and so forth
- do something for the bereaved.

End

The end phase is used to sum up what has taken place during the meeting, but also to plan what will happen in the time to come. The role of the class during the funeral can be discussed, and the class members can decide whether they want to have more meetings to go through what has happened. The intensity of the event will decide how important this is. If several students are dead, or a teacher died suddenly, this may necessitate several meetings – or using more class hours where the students can express their grief, for example through creative means.

A unified act or initiative on behalf of the class, such as the agreement to knit a carpet together or make a large drawing together for the bereaved, can be a nice ending to a meeting, and give the class a way of expressing care for those most involved.

At the end of the meeting, the children should be asked if there are any questions they want to ask, or something that is unclear. The children's experience of the meeting can also be enquired about.

Following the meeting it is easier to return to ordinary schoolwork again because the children have talked through what has happened.

What is needed over time is contingent on the scope of what has happened and what experiences the children have gone through. In relation to the sudden death of a student we have shown that many struggle over time (Dyregrov et al. 1999b). Unfortunately, many schools have a system that only includes follow-up in the first week until the burial/cremation is completed. Although not all students have a need for conversations over time, subgroups of children who are especially affected (i.e. good friends or those who witnessed a death) may need more follow-up. To ensure that children who struggle get the appropriate help after an event that strongly affected many children, a screening (systematic assessment) after about a month is advisable. Measures that can be helpful in such a screening may be found at www.childrenandwar.org.

During the meeting, teachers should notice whether any of the children are especially affected by what has happened, and make individual contact with them later. Teachers must also invite the children to contact them if they need to talk more about the death. The teacher also has to assess whether any children need therapeutic contact. If this seems necessary, the children's parents should be contacted.

Use of other expressive means

The classroom meeting uses words as the primary mean of expression. It is, however, of value to use other means of expression to assist children. This is especially valuable for younger children.

In latter years we have used what has been called 'soft' methods in the follow-up of crisis events. Although several of these are to be used within a therapeutic setting, they can be adapted to the school setting. These are practical tools that make it easy for children to express their experiences, impressions, thoughts and reactions. They span from systematic writing tasks via pictures that they easily can create a story for, to drawings where children can put colour to the feeling tone they experience and visual boxes where they can indicate when in the day they experience the most difficult thoughts or feelings. In relation to the tsunami in 2004 we made a workbook that contains many such 'soft' methods or activities. Although the web page www.barneombudet.no/cgi-bin/barneombudet/imaker?id=16755 is in Norwegian the visualizations may be worth looking at. Insert the address in your web-browser and click on 'Tsunami artbook'.

At the preschool age, reading from a book in the play group when the children are gathered together can be a good starting point for conversation and play. Literary texts and poems are useful with older children.

Use of colouring, painting, drawing and organized play is also helpful with younger children. Sand is well suited for burial-play, and material as toy crosses, toy chapels and so forth, should be available for the children.

Dramatic play can recreate events and help children 'tumble around' with what has happened. For children it can be important that they can invent other endings to the event, that is, that he or she did not die, or that they were able to save him or her. Where a death was caused by others, or was due to 'human error', children may find relief in drawing or playing out fantasies of revenge or punishment. The play can be specific to the event and very detailed, and it helps the children to get a grip on what has happened, as well as lessening their feelings of helplessness by giving them an after-the-fact control of what happened.

Songs can serve the same functions. In work with children in Uganda and Mozambique (see Dodge and Raundalen 1987), it was found that children have a remarkable ability to transform their experiences of trauma into song and dance play. In our work with refugee children who have sustained major losses, music and dance has been an integrated part of help (Raundalen, Lorentzen and Dyregrov 2005). Music therapy has been proven very useful in working with children and adolescents that experience psychological difficulties (Gold, Voracek and Wigram 2004).

Use of drawings can be supplemented by letting the children make a collection of clippings from newspapers and magazines. Here they can choose dramatic sequences that, together with drawings, can be used to create works that would not be possible separately. After serious accidents in which children have been involved, children can cut pictures of children in smaller parts to symbolize the body damage.

By using creative means and different non-verbal expressions, it is possible for children to achieve a reduction of tension, as well as making their thoughts and impressions concrete. This can take place while interacting with peers. Such activity is less influenced by defence mechanisms that may otherwise make the children avoid painful events and hinder cognitive and emotional work-through. At the same time, children express wishes, hopes and other feelings, but most of all this fosters integration of thoughts and feelings about what has happened. Klingman, Koenigsfeld and Markman (1987) give a good presentation of the use of creative expressive means in relation to a disaster where many schoolchildren were killed.

Visiting the scene of the event

After accidents or violent deaths a visit to the scene can help in understanding and comprehending an event. Besides helping us to confront reality and get a grip on what happened, the visit to the place where a friend or fellow student died also helps in letting feelings go.

If the class or group of friends collectively visit the place where a friend died it usually is helpful for them to give expression to their grief through a concrete act or ritual, such as placing a flower or something else on the place where it happened.

Visiting the bereaved parents

Some students want to visit the bereaved parents. For the bereaved parents this is a situation that evokes mixed emotions. They find that it feels good to be visited and to experience the support that friends and classmates show, but at the same time they are painfully reminded about the lost one. After the death they not only face the loss of their child, but the loss of life and activity in their home. The emptiness and quietness can be hard and intrusive, and even more so when they meet their child's friends. The meeting can trigger ambivalent feelings, and an intense longing for the lost one.

Usually both friends and parents feel that it is helpful to continue to have contact. Parents appreciate their child's friends continuing to visit, and the visits keep them, to some degree, in contact with their lost child. It can be helpful if the teacher contacts the bereaved parents to find out what they think about a visit from classmates – and to help make arrangements for such a visit.

Contact between school and home following a death

When a student dies, teachers are often unsure about how active they should be in contacting the home. Many think this will be an additional strain on the parents in an already difficult situation. Others do not know what to say or what to do, and wait until it no longer feels natural to make contact.

My experience is that parents usually appreciate very much being contacted by their child's teacher. The teacher can contact the parents both to convey his or her sympathy, as well as to prepare them for the classmates' wish to be present at the funeral. A home visit some days after the death, where the teacher sits down and talks with the parents, is highly valued by the parents. Some teachers have functioned as a primary source of support for parents following the death of a child.

When there are other schoolchildren in the family, the need for good contact between the parents and the school is evident. Unfortunately, it is my experience that many schoolchildren in grief experience a lack of understanding from both school and their teachers. It can be that teachers do not understand the grief reactions, especially the concentration difficulties, but also that they blame them for being absent from the rituals or professional follow-up. If a student is absent following a death, it is especially important to establish good communication with the home, to see if there is anything the teacher can do to help.

Commemorating the child

When a child has died it is best to let his or her desk remain empty throughout the school year. This marks the fact that the memory of the dead child is present in the classroom. Sometimes all reminders of the dead child are quickly removed from the classroom by well-intentioned adults. This takes away concrete connections and reminders for students' grief, and gives a negative signal to children about how much people mean to each other: 'Would my life mean as little as that if I died?', as all the possessions were quickly removed and another child soon took the dead child's place.

When the child's desk is removed from the classroom, this should happen in agreement with the class, and with the help of the students. The students should be prepared for the fact that the desk and chair will not be there at the start of a new school year.

At the end of the school year the child's death should be marked in a simple way, for example by the teacher saying some words or by having one of the students read a poem.

It will also be natural to talk about the child on his or her day of birth and day of death – this should not necessarily be a long conversation, but should be one to commemorate the child and talk about how he or she is missed. If a child died, a visit to the grave half a year and a year after the death, or on the child's birthday, can be followed by a conversation in the classroom. Individual follow-up is undertaken if indicated, and if several students continue to experience difficulties, a group (crisis or grief group) can be started.

If it is a child who has lost one or both parents, the teacher should be aware of the extra pain that such children may feel on Mother's Day or Father's Day. This awareness can prevent him or her from feeling extra lonely when other children make or buy presents for their parents. Talking with the student in advance, and recognition of his or her loss in the classroom, may be called for.

Handling death in the play group

How a death is dealt with in the play group will depend on the type of death. If it is the anticipated death of a child due to an illness, it will be best if the staff use occasions to prepare the children for what will happen. This can be done through the use of books that are read to the children, or by talking about death in relation to seeing dead animals, insects or plants. Preparatory discussions about less threatening aspects of dying and death can increase children's understanding of what is happening. Interaction with local health personnel is important in these circumstances, and it can be helpful to get advice from health professionals about different aspects of illness and prognosis, which is important in caring for the group of children.

When death happens as a result of illness, preschool children need to discuss illness and treatment and learn about these. When, for example, a child with cancer loses his or her hair as a consequence of chemotherapy, the other children need to be reassured that they will not lose their hair. The difference between dangerous and non-dangerous illnesses needs to be explained. Assurances and information that when children get sick it is almost always with non-dangerous diseases must also be given. When a child dies in spite of treatment, it must be emphasized that everything that could be done was done, that the child was not alone when he or she died and that he or she did not feel pain.

Play material such as bandages, syringes and other material for free play is very helpful to children in giving them the opportunity to work through the feelings that serious illness or death may evoke. In their play they choose different roles, from doctor to parent, and most often the doctor is able to cure the sick.

When a death happens, be it sudden or anticipated, the children in a play group have to be told. Preschool children need an explanation of what happened that is given with simple words adjusted to their age. They may need to sit on someone's lap while being told what happened and why. Owing to their immature concept formation we need to check what they have understood to prevent misunderstandings. A calm and safe context with physical closeness is very important for this group, followed by good advice to parents on how they can care for their children at home. This, among other things, includes accepting more clinging and temporary sleeping in their parents' bed and keeping routines at home as usual as possible. It is possible to give some simple information to the children:

> 'Sometimes we become sad, angry or afraid after someone dies. Then you can go to Mama or Papa or to one of us here in the kindergarten and we can support you and talk about what you feel. If you think scary thoughts that make you afraid, you can let good, strong thoughts take away the scary thoughts. Strong thoughts are thoughts like "Mama and Papa will be there to comfort me", "I will think of something nice". You can also think of your favourite cartoon.'

Before children are given information it is best to have a meeting for the parents where they and the staff can discuss the situation together. Sometimes it is not possible to delay telling the children until such a meeting is held. The children will overhear adults talk about what has happened, and we know that information is rapidly spread throughout the child network, and so are fantasies and anxiety. It is important that parents learn about what has been said in the play group. A short letter to the home, informing them about the situation, is appropriate.

Information given to the children must be trustworthy and concrete to lay the foundation for taking care of the children's needs in the near future. The death of a child will usually result in many questions and comments in the following weeks, and at the same time the children will play out different aspects of the event. The same questions may be repeated several times over:

'Why didn't the doctor give her more medicine?'

'Can we get cancer and die?'

'Can you die in an accident?'

'Are feet cold, down in the grave?'

When the children repeatedly ask the same questions, they also seem to check whether the answers they get are the same. Often, questions and conversations will centre on the fact that the dead person will not come back or will not play any more, and on why this could not be prevented. Without a concrete answer the children will fill in the blanks with their own misunderstandings and fantasies, and these will often be spread among the children.

When there is a dramatic death, or some other death has a serious impact on the group (e.g. the death of one of the primary day care staff), a meeting with the parents is always called for. The content of this meeting will vary with the situation, but it should provide the following:

- information about the event

- information about how this has been handled in the play group

- giving parents an opportunity to express their reactions, and learn what has been discussed in the children's homes

- concrete advice about how they can deal with the death at home, with suggestions about books they can read to learn more about children's reactions, or books to read with their children

- discussion on how to handle the event in the play group in the weeks to come.

The parents' meeting can actively promote mutual support, as well as stimulate plans about how to help the bereaved. It gives the parents an opportunity to work through their own reactions. These often take the form of increased vulnerability and fear that something similar might happen to their own child.

As in schools, it is important to provide concrete support for children's grief work. This means that clothes, the child's picture and locker and so on should be part of the other children's environment for a while. In addition, children can look at pictures they have in the play group, or borrow or make copies from those the family have. If a child's parent(s) are able to, they may visit the play group and meet the children. This can be a meaningful experience both for the bereaved parents, and for the children, who may have many questions. If parents are to make such a visit, they must be prepared for the children's questions.

Children may be present at the funeral together with their parents, but this should take place with the understanding of the bereaved parents. At the funeral the children may give concrete expression to their grief, as described earlier. It also helps the children if the group can visit the child's grave collectively.

Chapter Nine

Crisis- or grief-therapy for children

As a ground rule, children in grief should be helped by parents or caregivers who, through their sensitivity and closeness, can facilitate children's thoughts and feelings. This means that the recovery environment of grieving children will accept their grief and have patience with it over time. Most children are resilient and will adjust to a loss without any professional bereavement intervention. Overall results from reviews of bereavement interventions do not indicate that such interventions have a significant influence on adjustment (Currier, Holland and Neimeyer 2007). However, many events are so sudden, so dramatic, or of such extreme nature, that the children's needs are best taken care of if the family seeks or receives early professional assistance. Some children will, despite the best immediate follow-up from their close surroundings, need follow-up from competent professionals. Early help reduces the likelihood of chronic or delayed grief, as well as the chance of developing post-traumatic stress reactions.

Among the events where early professional contact are advisable are:

- when a child is bereaved by suicide or murder

- when the child witnesses a death

- where the child had responsibility for the death or responsibility for the dead person (such as when siblings are babysitting a child who dies of a crib death) or were with the person who died.

Parents or the remaining parent can obtain advice from professionals who help them to take care of children's needs, and parents and professionals together can assess if a child needs individual follow-up. In situations where children show strong anticipatory grief reactions, strong immediate grief reactions, chronic grief or change their personality, contact should be made with professionals.

When a child or a parent dies, parents or the remaining parent almost always experience strong grief reactions that will have an impact on children. Early professional help for parents is often the best way to reduce the chance of unnecessary long-term problems in the family. Such problems often show up in the child sub-system. Some of the best help that can be given in such situations is to give help to children's carers.

Children may need professional help with both the immediate effects of a death and the after-effects. Loss during childhood that is not worked through can hamper personality development and lead to psychological problems later in life. Early crisis intervention (with the establishment of contact close to the event) can help the child to work through feelings and thoughts, and to express and accept their grief.

In other situations, contact is first established after the development of symptoms or problems that parents or schools cannot handle. Such problems develop even if the guidelines outlined in this book are followed, and it is important that adults do not delay too long before contacting professionals for advice, for example if they find that the child's character has changed (if he or she isolates themself or becomes aggressive) or he or she develops problems in keeping up with schoolwork. Unfortunately, some parents and teachers delay too long until they seek professional advice, as they think the problems will disappear, or because they do not register the problems the child is experiencing.

Below are some aspects that may indicate that a child needs further help:

- the child isolates him- or herself from friends and adults
- school performance is seriously affected
- the child's behaviour is drastically changed and the changes continue over time
- strong reactions continue over time
- the child develops phobic reactions
- the child talks about hurting him- or herself or commiting suicide
- the child harbours lasting strong guilt feelings
- the child constantly ruminates about what has happened.

If reactions continue unabated over the first weeks, or the reactions increase in intensity as time goes by, it may also be cause for contacting professionals. Other circumstances that may indicate that professional help is needed include the child's daily function being impaired or clearly reduced. Often these aspects appear jointly making it easy to recognize the student in need for more help. It is more difficult with quiet students who may suffer on the inside but not show much on the outside, or students with a high degree of avoidance who grow increasingly phobic (avoiding everything associated with what happened), who are apparently not bothered by what happened as they become experts in avoiding. Because this leads to a large expenditure of mental energy, but little efficiency in schoolwork, it is important to monitor the student's level of functioning at school when deciding if extra help is needed. Often, such students suffer sleep difficulties, leading to school absence, and good contact with the home can help in identifying and reducing problems at an early stage. It is obvious that such situations require sensitive teacher eyes to identify the child's problems.

When children are having problems following a death, this is often caused by not having worked through the traumatic aspects of the event, and this interferes with the progression of the normal grief reaction. But it can also be caused by the child being lonely in his or her grief; they may have difficulty talking about what has happened, or the sorrow may be so strong that parents do not get through to them. Such reactions necessitate short-term therapeutic intervention, in the form of either individual or family therapy, according to the character of the event or the reactions. In certain cases, long-term therapy is necessary. Without giving a thorough coverage of grief therapy for children, some general comments on therapy with children in grief are offered below.

The core of therapy with young children will most often be play. Play gives children the opportunity to express themselves through action rather than words. This does not mean that younger children should not be given information and be helped to gain 'insight', but through the help of play material (sandbox, houses, dolls and other play and drawing materials) the child can gradually express different reactions and thoughts related to the death. Through careful interpretation by the therapist, the child's indirect (symbolic) and direct signals of central themes and feelings may be dealt with in the therapy hours. At the same time the child is allowed to express aggressive fantasies (thoughts of revenge), guilt feelings or other feelings that are difficult to put into words.

Somewhat older children will undo the death in fantasy and play, and in this way counteract the traumatic helplessness. It can be helpful to comment on the traumatic elements that are evident in their drawings or play: 'I am sure you would have wished your brother to live', 'I guess you have thought a lot about taking revenge on the fellow who drove the car'. Such comments can result in a strong abreaction in a child, a reaction that needs to be met with security and acceptance by the therapist, but at the same time in such a manner that the child is helped not to be emotionally overwhelmed. The core of the traumatic death can be approached by asking the child: 'What was the worst thing about what happened?'

Older children may also use expressive means, such as dramatic play and creative activities, but generally the use of words in expressing themselves will become more important. The establishment of trust between therapist and client is essential for the child to dare to put thoughts, fantasies and feelings into words. The therapist's activity will vary between listening and interpreting, explaining, teaching and making the different reactions the child exhibits understandable. Trust, understanding and respect are key words in the contact. But confronting can also be an important part of trauma work. The therapist helps the child to encounter memories and places of importance for the grief process. This may be a visit to the scene of an accident or crime, or a visit to the hospital to see the place where the child's mother or father died or was brought when he or she died. Confronting can also mean a meeting with one of the people present at the scene of the event, or facing difficult reminders or grief stimuli.

When intrusive memories and anxiety are manifest as strong reactions, children can benefit from learning simple relaxation techniques – and methods that stop such thoughts (thought-stopping techniques). In cases where the child has been a witness to, or has been involved in, a trauma situation, different forms of antiphobic training or more specific anxiety-management techniques can be of help. Direct work to teach the child to control intrusive recollections may be required.

It is important that follow-up is initiated early after traumatic deaths, before different protection mechanisms have interfered with trauma recovery. Personality changes and changes in the child's ability to handle feelings can take place, and hamper adequate working-through of the event. An early therapeutic alliance is helpful when long-term follow-up is necessary. Although this book emphasizes how adults – parents, teachers and others – can help children in grief and reduce the likelihood of long-term problems, some deaths are so devastating that they can lead to long-term problems regardless of how they are handled. Not all problems can be dealt with by a teacher, and all symptoms do not disappear with understanding and concern. Do not wait before contacting a professional for advice.

Parallel with the development of specific treatment methods for post-traumatic stress disorder (PTSD), more specific treatment for complicated grief is being developed. Alongside the gradual establishment of a new diagnostic category called 'prolonged grief disorder' (Prigerson, Vanderwerker and Maciejewski, in press) therapy methods that are aimed specifically at children who suffer complicated grief, sometimes called 'childhood traumatic grief', are being developed (see Cohen and Mannarino 2004; Cohen, Mannarino and Knudsen 2004; Cohen, Mannarino and Staron 2006; Lieberman et al. 2003). Preliminary evidence indicates that complicated grief is also a clinically significant syndrome in children and adolescents (Melhem *et al.* 2007). If the child harbours strong post-traumatic reactions following a death, aiming resources at these problems early on is deemed important, as such reactions hamper usual grief reactions. The design of programmes to assist children who experience problems over time should include both focus on features of their experience that are unique, that is, the type of death they have experienced, as well as features that focus on processes that are common among children across different dimensions.

Chapter Ten

Bereavement groups
for children

There are many bereavement self-help groups for adults. Such groups are a good supplement to support from family and networks, and eventual professional support. Such groups help to normalize reactions, develop cohesion, stimulate hope and sort out thoughts. They also provide good opportunities for the expression of thoughts and feelings. In addition, they can prepare the bereaved for the reactions and problems they are likely to face.

Groups for children are more rare. In the USA, such groups are used in different places (see Masterman and Reams 1988; Zambelli *et al.* 1988). Children's groups have been of help for children who have themselves been involved in dramatic accidents, or have witnessed the death of others, for example the capsize of the ferry *Herald of Free Enterprise* near Zeebrügge in 1987 (Yule and Williams 1990) or the earthquake in Armenia in 1988 (Goenjian *et al.* 1997). More recently Layne and co-workers (2001) developed a group programme for adolescents who have experienced loss and violence in the inner cities of the USA. In 20 consecutive weeks the participants meet at school for 50-minute sessions in groups of five to seven at the ages of 11 to 14. Participants are screened to include those who had experienced trauma and loss, evidencing strong reactions as a consequence. Both trauma and loss are focused in the groups. In addition to fostering group cohesion and coping strategies, working through traumatic events, fostering adaptive grief and a normal grief progression are emphasized. Evaluation of this programme showed that those who participated improved regarding post-traumatic stress reactions, complicated grief reactions and school performance.

In contrast to adults, children like an opportunity to play uncommittedly or be with others who have been in the same situation as themselves, without the group having a structured agenda all the time. In a meta-analytic review of the effectiveness of bereavement interventions with children, Currier *et al.* (2007) found that 12 of the 13 studies they reviewed consisted of group approaches. Their conclusion was that the data did not support the general helpfulness of these treatments. However, these authors also reflect that the reason these approaches were of little value may be because too much time had passed from the child's loss to the beginning of the intervention, and that most studies failed to screen for those with a genuine need for follow-up. It should also be noted that these interventions were generally not instigated at schools. Usually, if participants in a grief group (or their parents) are asked how they view the groups they are very positive (Karpatschof 2002).

In the group children can express their reactions and learn that others have had similar experiences, and they can compare different ways of handling difficult situations, for example how to deal with sleeping difficulties. In the group established after the *Herald of Free Enterprise* disaster, the children agreed to use 'Walkman' cassette players to fill the quiet surrounding bedtime, which otherwise was filled with thoughts that triggered anxiety (Yule and Williams 1990).

Bereavement groups for children can be very helpful, but adults should be careful that members do not build a new identity around their grief, and be aware that such groups can sometimes become destructive without direction, or that some 'compulsive talkers' export their way of resolving their grief to others or dominate the group too much. A child mental health professional should be involved in managing such a group. Setting up grief groups at the school led by school nurses whom have received good training in both usual grief reactions, signs of complicated grief and screening for those, and group leadership can be an important service to ensure that grieving children are well cared for.

Chapter Eleven

Caring for oneself

—◆—

Both teachers and others who help people in grief will have the experience that they can react themselves, as they are exposed to grief and despair at close hand. Many will experience reactions that are parallel to those of the bereaved: sadness, anger, helplessness and anxiety can all be experienced by the helpers. When children experience the death of someone they love, we react more strongly than when adults go through such a situation. Especially in the kindergarten with all the physical contact, the staff feel very close to the children. When preschool children die it affects the staff profoundly. But also, following other deaths that educational staff work in close relation to can lead to emotional strain. We identify more with a child, more easily make their grief our own, and find it more difficult to stop thinking about what has happened. When children are the victims, it touches our own vulnerability more strongly. We become afraid something will happen to our own children, and we may feel especially helpless at not being able to do enough for the child. Sometimes this feeling can result in too little respect for the child's right to be given time to be alone, or to be allowed to grieve.

Work with people in grief can also trigger thoughts about existential questions, both questions about meaning and justice, and our own fear of dying. Children's grief can also touch our own fear of separation and loss, as we experienced these in childhood. These are matters that it is important to know about if we are to help children in grief, and they should be thought about before engaging in giving help to children. It is helpful to have reflected over our own losses, so that we do not load potential unfinished grief on to the children. Sometimes it is best to let others take care of the help and follow-up.

It is easy to become sad or depressed if a student dies or loses his or her parents. Our capacity to help is closely tied to our capacity to understand and show empathy. But at the same time this makes us vulnerable. As a helper it is of no use to try to shut out or hide our own feelings – it is all right for the children to see us shed some tears, but a total breakdown may create much anxiety.

It is helpful, when engaging in helping children in grief, to have a security net of good colleagues around, as well as steady support at home. The use of support people to whom we can express our own impressions and reactions is good self-care, and makes us better equipped to handle similar tasks in the future.

Good self-care should include the expectation of own reactions. It is an advantage to have some knowledge about the reactions that helpers face in work with grief and crises (see Dyregrov and Mitchell 1992; Dyregrov, Mitchell and Hordvik 1995; Rothschild and Rand 2006) because this helps us interpret and accept our own reactions. Good self-care includes seeking out others to share impressions and reactions, and being able to allow others to support and care for us. It can also be useful to confront the stressors we face, by allowing ourself to think about, and give words to, our experiences. After working in close contact with a dramatic situation, it may be necessary to go through the event in a more detailed manner.

Talking with our partner, a close friend or colleague can be invaluable following such work. If the event has included several adults as helpers, a group work-through may be called for.

Good self-care is a *sine qua non* for being able to provide good help and support the next time a child or an adult in our vicinity experiences grief or crisis.

Self-care

Some important points in self-care are:

- Learn about reactions that may be experienced by helpers who work with grief or crisis.

- Anticipate that you will experience emotional reactions if you are supporting children in grief or crisis; usually these reactions will decline over the subsequent days or weeks.

- Use your partner, a good friend or a colleague to talk about the strain you experience.

- Remember that you cannot carry the child's grief for him or her, but you can help or support the child to express his or her grief.

- Be careful not to take on too much at the same time.

- Have someone you can share the responsibility with, or someone you can seek advice from.

- Contact professionals if an event has shaken up both you and others. It can then be useful to arrange a meeting where you go through your impressions and reactions in detail (a psychological debriefing meeting; see Dyregrov 2002).

- Remember that to be of help to the child, you need to take good care of yourself.

Peer support

You can be of good help and give good peer support to somebody who helps a child in grief by:

- knowing about reactions in such situations

- actively contacting the person and being willing to listen and talk to him or her, and by acknowledging the feelings and thoughts that are expressed

- offering your company, without being intrusive

- having patience, and accepting that many need to talk extensively about their involvement

- refraining from phrases such as: 'It could have been worse', 'Time heals all wounds', 'You will feel better tomorrow' and so forth

- anticipating that a person engaged in such a task may not have full working capacity, and might need someone to ease his or her normal workload for a period

- tactfully advising him or her to seek professional advice if it is obvious that he or she has problems dealing with the situation on their own.

For those who want to understand helper's reactions more deeply there are several books that describe such aspects: Figley (2002); Rothschild and Rand (2006); and Stamm (1995).

Grief in children – guidelines for care

___

Open and honest communication
- give age-adjusted explanations
- reduce confusion
- refrain from abstract explanations
- do not explain death as 'a voyage' or 'sleep'

Give time for cognitive mastery
- allow questions and conversations
- accept short conversations
- look at albums, photographs and videos
- let the children visit the grave, but do not put pressure on the child
- accept children's play related to the death

Make the loss real
- let the child participate in rituals (seeing the dead, funeral)
- do not hide your own feelings
- keep reminders of the dead person present

Stimulate emotional coping

- work for continuity in home, school or play group
- avoid unnecessary separations
- talk with children about their anxiety about something happening to their parents or themselves
- talk with children about eventual guilt feelings
- acknowledge and normalize the child's reactions; do not minimize or reject them
- conversations throughout childhood help the child build an inner representation of the dead loved one that they can keep through life
- if the child is sad, provide hope that it will become better but also tell them that it can take time

Stimulate expression of thoughts and feelings

- make a memorial album, put together pictures, poems, add writing and so on
- drawing, painting, paper clippings and suchlike
- write a letter to the deceased
- write poems, sentence completion, 'The worst that happened was…'
- role-play, dramatic reconstruction, make a video, puppet play
- rituals at visiting the grave or the site of the event

Resources

Internet websites with information about children, adolescents and families in grief

- The Compassionate Friends: an organization offering support and encouragement to others after the death of a child.
  (www.tcf.org.uk/leaflets/lesurviving.html)

- Roadcare: a website to help people who have been bereaved as a result of a road traffic accident.
  (www.cadd.org.uk/docs/CADDCoping.pdf)

- The Childhood Bereavement Network is a national federation working with bereaved children and young people.
  (www.childhoodbereavementnetwork.org.uk/haad_about_bereavement_childhood_cr.htm)

- The Child Bereavement Charity: by listening to bereaved children and parents, The Child Bereavement Charity aims to improve the care offered by professionals to grieving families in the immediate crisis and in the many months following the death of someone important in their lives.
  (www.childbereavement.org.uk)

- Cruse Bereavement Care: a website to promote the well-being of bereaved people.
  (www.crusebereavementcare.org.uk)

- RD4U (Road for You): a website designed for young people by young people. It is part of Cruse Bereavement Care's Youth Involvement Project and is intended to support people after the death of someone close. (www.rd4u.org.uk)

- Winston's Wish: helps bereaved children and young people rebuild their lives after a family death. They offer practical support and guidance to families, professionals and anyone concerned about a grieving child. (www.winstonswish.org.uk)

- Resources for Children Experiencing Grief: a resource guide created in order to make materials available to adults essential in the lives of children experiencing grief. (www.kidsgrief.com/index.html)

- Growthhouse: a website devoted to helping children and youn adults work through grief and serious illness. (www.growthhouse.org/childgrv.html)

Resources and contingency plans for schools

- A disaster and crisis management guidebook (www.ncef.org/pubs/edfacilities-disaster-management-guidebook-2007.pdf)

- A model school crisis management plan (www.doe.virginia.gov/VDOE/Instruction/model.html)

- A resource list for disaster preparedness and response for schools and universities (www.edfacilities.org/rl/disaster.cfm)

- Practical suggestions for educators (www.nasponline.org/resources/crisis_safety/neat_poland.aspx)

- School emergency planning (www.ed.gov/admins/lead/safety/emergencyplan/index.html)

Disaster plans in general

- Examples of disaster plans
  (http://sul-server-2.stanford.edu/bytopic/disasters/plans)

Books about loss which can be read to children

Grandad's Ashes
Walter Smith
Jessica Kingsley Publishers

Children Also Grieve
Talking About Death and Healing
Linda Goldman
Jessica Kingsley Publishers

Always and Forever
Alan Durant
Illustrated by Debi Gliori
Corgi Children's Books

Granpa
John Burningham
Red Fox

What on Earth Do You Do when Someone Dies?
Trevor Romain and Elizabeth Verdick
Free Spirit Publishing Inc.

Badger's Parting Gifts
Susan Varley
Picture Lions

When Dinosaurs Die: a Guide to Understanding Death
Laurene Krasny Brown and Marc Brown
Little, Brown and Company

Michael Rosen's Sad Book
Michael Rosen
Illustrated by Quentin Blake
Walker Books Ltd

The Day the Sea Went Out and Never Came Back
Margot Sunderland
Illustrated by Nicky Armstrong
Speechmark

Helping Children with Loss: A Guidebook
Margot Sunderland
Illustrated by Nicky Armstrong
Speechmark

References

Adam, K.S., Lohrenz, J.G., Harper, D. and Streiner, D. (1982) 'Early parental loss and suicidal ideation in university students.' *Canadian Journal of Psychiatry 27*, 275–281.

Bergen, M. (1958) 'Effect of severe trauma on a 4-year-old child.' *Psychoanalytic Study of the Child 13*, 407–429.

Black, D. and Urbanowicz, M.A. (1987) 'Family intervention with bereaved children.' *Journal of Child Psychology and Psychiatry 28*, 467–476.

Bohanek, J.G., Marin, K.A., Fivush, R. and Duke, M.P. (2006). 'Family narrative interaction and children's sense of self.' *Family Process 45*, 39–54.

Bowlby, J. (1980) *Attachment and Loss. Volume III.* New York, NY: Basic Books.

Brent, D.A., Moritz, G., Bridge, J., Perper, J. and Canobbio, R. (1996) 'The impact of adolescent suicide on siblings and parents: a longitudinal follow-up.' *Suicide and Life-threatening Behaviour 26*, 253–259.

Broberg, A.O., Dyregrov, A. and Lilled, L. (2005) 'The Göteborg discotheque fire – posttraumatic stress, and school adjustment as reported by the primary victims 18 months later.' *Journal of Child Psychology and Psychiatry 46*, 1279–1286.

Brown, A.C., Sandler, I.N., Tein, J-Y., Liu, X. and Haine, R.A. (2007) 'Implications of parental suicide and violent death for promotion of resilience of parentally-bereaved children.' *Death Studies 31*, 301–335.

Bruce, M. (2006) 'A systematic and conceptual review of posttraumatic stress in childhood cancer survivors and their parents.' *Clinical Psychology Review 26,* 233–256.

Campbell, S. and Silverman, P. (1996) *Widower; when men are left alone.* Amityville, NY: Baywood Publishing.

Cerel, J., Fristad, M.A., Verducci, J., Weller, R.A. and Weller, E.B. (2006) 'Childhood bereavement: psychopathology in the 2 years postparental death.' *Journal of the American Academy of Child and Adolescent Psychiatry 45,* 681–690.

Cerel, J., Fristad, M.A., Weller, E.B. and Weller, R.A. (1999) 'Suicide–bereaved children and adolescents: a controlled longitudinal examination.' *Journal of the American Academy of Child and Adolescent Psychiatry 38,* 672–679.

Christ, G.H., Siegel, K., Freund, B., Langosch, D., Hendersen, S., Sperber, D. and Weinstein, L. (1993) 'Impact of parental terminal cancer on latency–age children.' *American Journal of Orthopsychiatry 63,* 417–425.

Cohen, J.A. and Mannarino, A.P. (2004) 'Treatment of childhood traumatic grief.' *Journal of Clinical Child and Adolescent Psychiatry 33,* 819–831.

Cohen, J.A., Mannarino, A.P., Greenberg, T., Padlo, S. and Shipley, C. (2002) 'Childhood traumatic grief.' *Trauma, Violence and Abuse 3,* 307–327.

Cohen, J.A., Mannarino, A.P. and Knudsen, K. (2004) 'Treating childhood traumatic grief: a pilot study.' *Journal of American Academy of Child and adolescent psychiatry 43,* 1225–1233.

Cohen, J.A., Mannarino, A.P. and Staron, V.R. (2006) 'A pilot study of modified cognitive-behavioral therapy for childhood traumatic grief (CBT-CTG).' *Journal of the American Academy of Child and Adolescent Psychiatry 45,* 1465–1473.

Corr, C.A. and Corr, D.M. (1996) (eds) *Handbook of childhood death and bereavement.* New York, NY: Springer Publishing Company.

Cuddy-Casey, M. and Orvaschel, H. (1997) 'Children's understanding of death in relation to child suicidality and homicidality.' *Clinical Psychology Review 17,* 33–45.

Currier, J.M., Holland, J.M. and Neimeyer, R.A. (2007) 'The effectiveness of bereavement interventions with children: a meta-analytic review of controlled outcome research.' *Journal of Clinical Child and Adolescent Psychology 36,* 253–259.

Denes-Raj, V. and Ehrlichman, H. (1991) 'Effects of premature parental death on subjective life expectancy, death anxiety, and health behavior.' *Omega 23*, 309–321.

Diamond, L.M. and Aspinwall, L.G. (2003) 'Emotion regulation across the life span: an integrative perspective emphasizing self-regulation, positive affect, and dyadic processes.' *Motivation and Emotion 27*, 125–156.

Dodge, C. and Raundalen, M. (1987) (eds) *War, Violence and Children in Uganda*. Oslo: University Press, Oslo.

Dowdney, L. (2000) 'Childhood bereavement following parental death.' *Journal of Psychology and Psychiatry 41*, 819–830.

Dyregrov, A. (1988) 'The loss of a child: the sibling's perspective.' In R. Kumar and I.F. Brockington (eds) *Motherhood and Mental Illness 2*. London: Wright.

Dyregrov, A. (1990) 'Parental reactions to the loss of an infant child: A review.' *Scandinavian Journal of Psychology 31*, 266–280.

Dyregrov, A. (2001a) 'Telling the truth or hiding the facts. An evaluation of current strategies for assisting children following adverse events.' *Association for Child Psychology and Psychiatry Occasional papers 17*, 25–38.

Dyregrov, A. (2001b) 'Early intervention – a family perspective.' *Advances in Mind–Body Medicine 17*, 9–17.

Dyregrov, A. (2002). *Psychological Debriefing. A Leader's Guide for Small Group Crisis Intervention*. Ellicott City, MD: Chevron Publishing Company.

Dyregrov, A. (2004) 'Educational consequences of loss and trauma.' *Educational and Child Psychology 21*, 77–84.

Dyregrov, A., Bie Wikander, A.M. and Vigerust, S. (1999b) 'Sudden death of a classmate and friend. Adolescents' perception of support from their school.' *School Psychology International 20*, 191–208.

Dyregrov, A., Frykholm, A-M., Lilled, L., Broberg, A. and Holmberg, I. (2003) 'The Göteborg discothèque fire 1998.' *Scandinavian Journal of Psychology 44*, 449–457.

Dyregrov, A., Gjestad, R., Bie Wikander, A.M. and Vigerust, S. (1999a) 'Reactions following the sudden death of a classmate.' *Scandinavian Journal of Psychology 40*, 167–176.

Dyregrov, A., Gupta, L., Gjestad, R. and Raundalen, M. (2002) 'Is the culture always right?' *Traumatology 8*, 3–10.

Dyregrov, A., Matthiesen, S.B., Kristoffersen, J.I. and Mitchell, J.T. (1994) 'Gender differences in adolescents' reactions to the murder of their teacher.' *Journal of Adolescent Research 9*, 363–383.

Dyregrov, A. and Mitchell, J.T. (1992) 'Work with traumatized children – psychological effects and coping strategies.' *Journal of Traumatic Stress 5*, 5–17.

Dyregrov, A., Mitchell, J.T. and Hordvik, E. (1995) 'When a child dies: Helping the helpers.' In T. Rognum (ed.): *Sudden Infant Death Syndrome. New Trends in the Nineties.* Oslo: Scandinavian University Press.

Dyregrov, A. and Yule, W. (2006) 'A review of PTSD in children. A commissioned review.' *Child and Adolescent Mental Health 11*, 176–184.

Dyregrov, K. (2006). 'Skolens viktige rolle etter selvmord.' *Bedre skole 1*, 46–51.

Dyregrov, K. and Dyregrov, A. (2004) 'Helping the family following suicide.' In B. Monroe and F. Kraus (eds), *Brief Interventions with Bereaved Children* (pp.201–215). Oxford: Oxford University Press.

Dyregrov, K. and Dyregrov, A. (2005) 'Siblings after suicide –"the forgotten bereaved".' *Suicide and Life Threatening Behaviour 35*, 714–724.

Feijo, L., Hernandez-Reif, M., Field, T., Burns, W., Valley-Gray, S. and Simco, E (2006) 'Mothers' depressed mood and anxiety levels are reduced after massaging their preterm infants.' *Infant Behavior and Development 29*, 476–480.

Field, T., Seligman, S., Scafidi, F. and Schanberg, S. (1996) 'Alleviating posttraumatic stress in children following hurricane Andrew.' *Journal of Applied Developmental Psychology 17*, 37–50.

Figley, C.R. (ed.) (2002) *Treating Compassion Fatigue.* New York, NY: Brunner–Routledge.

Forrest, G., Plumb, C., Ziebland, S. and Stein, A. (2006) 'Breast cancer in the family – children's perceptions of their mother's cancer and its initial treatment: qualitative study.' *British Medical Journal 332*, 998–1003.

Gold, C., Voracek, M. and Wigram, T. (2004) 'Effects of music therapy for children and adolescents with psychopathology: a meta-analysis.' *Journal of Child Psychology and Psychiatry 45*, 1054–1063.

Goenjian, A.K., Karayan, I., Pynoos, R.S., Minassian, D., Najarian, L.M., Steinberg, A.M. and Fairbanks, L.A. (1997) 'Outcome of psychotherapy among early adolescents after trauma.' *American Journal of Psychiatry 154*, 536–542.

Haine, R.A., Wolchik, S.A., Sandler, I.N., Millsap, R.E. and Ayers, T.S. (2006) 'Positive parenting as a protective resource for parentally bereaved children.' *Death Studies 30*, 1–28.

Harley, K. and Reese, E. (1999) 'Origins of autobiographical memory.' *Developmental Psychology 35*, 1338–1348.

Hogan, N.S. and DeSantis, L. (1996) 'Basic constructs of a theory of adolescent sibling bereavement.' In D. Klass, P.R. Silverman, and S.L. Nickman (eds) *Continuing Bonds: New Understandings of Grief.* Bristol, PA: Taylor & Francis.

Hogan, N.S. and Greenfield, D.B. (1991) 'Adolescent sibling bereavement symptomatology in a large community sample.' *Journal of Adolescent Research 6*, 97–113.

Hughes, P., Turton, P., Hopper, E. and McGauley, G.A. (2001) 'Disorganised attachment behaviour among infants born subsequent to stillbirth.' *Journal of Child Psychology and Psychiatry, 42*, 791–801.

Jacobsen, A. (1989) *Det var en gang vi ikke var her.* København: Hans Reitzels forlag.

John, O.P. and Gross, J.J. (2004) 'Healthy and unhealthy emotion regulation: Personality processes, individual differences, and life span development.' *Journal of Personality 77*, 1301–1334.

Kaplow, J.B., Saxe, G.N., Putnam, F.W., Pynoos, R.S. and Lieberman, A.F. (2006) 'The long-term consequences of early childhood trauma: a case study and discussion.' *Psychiatry 69*, 362–375.

Karpatschof, B. (ed.) (2002) *Når sorgens fugle flyver bort.* København: Egmont Fondens Støtte-og bevillingsadministrasjon.

Kaufman, K.R. and Kaufman, N.D. (2006) 'And then the dog died.' *Death Studies 30*, 61–76.

Klingman, A. (1987) A school-based emergency crisis intervention in a mass school disaster. *Professional Psychology: Research and Practice 18*, 604–612.

Klingman, A., Koenigsfeld, E. and Markman, D. (1987) 'Art activity with children following disaster: a preventive-oriented crisis intervention modality.' *The Arts in Psychotherapy 14*,153–166.

Kreicbergs, U., Valdimarsdottir, U., Onelöw, E., Henter, J-I. and Steinebeck, G. (2004) 'Talking about death with children who have severe malignant disease.' *The New England Journal of Medicine 351*, 1175–1186.

Landsdown, R., Frangoulis, S. and Jordan, N. (1997) 'Children's concept of an afterlife.' *Bereavement Care 16*, 16–19.

La Greca, A.M., Silverman, W.K., Vernberg, E.M. and Roberts, M.C. (eds) (2002) *Helping Children Cope with Disasters and Terrorism.* Washington, DC: American Psychological Association.

Layne, C.M., Pynoos, R.S., Salzman, W.R., Arslanagi, B., Savjak, N. et. al. (2001) 'Trauma/grief-focused group psychotherapy school-based postwar intervention with traumatized Bosnian adolescents.' *Group Dynamics: Theory, Research and Practice 5*, 277–290.

LeDoux, J. (1998) *The Emotional Brain.* New York, NY: Touchstone.

Lever, J. (1976) 'Sex differences in the games children play.' *Social Problems, 23*, 478–487.

Lieberman, A.F., Compton, N.C., Van Horn, P. and Ippen, C.G. (2003) *Losing a Parent to Death in the Early Years. Guidelines for the Treatment of Traumatic Bereavement in Infancy and Early Childhood.* Washington, DC: Zero to three Press.

Mack, K.Y. (2001) 'Childhood family disruptions and adult well-being: the differential effects of divorce and parental death.' *Death Studies 25*, 419–443.

Masterman, S.H. and Reams, R. (1988) 'Support groups for bereaved preschool and school-age children.' *American Journal of Orthopsychiatry 58*, 562–570.

McCown, D.E. (1984) 'Funeral attendance, cremation, and young siblings.' *Death Education 8*, 349–363.

Melhem, N.M., Moritz, G., Walker, M., Shear, M.K. and Brent, D. (2007) 'Phenomenology and correlates of complicated grief in children and adolescents.' *Journal of American Academy of Child and Adolescent Psychiatry 46*, 493–499.

Mitchell, J.T. (1983) 'When disaster strikes...the Critical Incident Stress debriefing process.' *Journal of Emergency Medical Services 8*, 36–39.

Nader, K. and Pynoos, R. (1993) 'School disaster: planning and initial interventions.' *Journal of Social Behavior and Personality 8*, 299–320.

Neimeyer, R.A. (ed.) (2000) *Lessons of Loss. A Guide to Coping.* Memphis, TN: Center for the Study of Loss and Transition.

Nickman, S.L. Silverman, P.R. and Normand, C. (1998) 'Children's construction of a deceased parent: the surviving parent's contribution.' *American Journal of Orthopsychiatry 68*, 126–134.

Otto, M.W., Henin, A., Hirshfeld-Becker, D.R., Pollack, M.H., Biederman, J. and Rosenbaum, J.F. (2007) 'Posttraumatic stress disorder symptoms following media exposure to tragic events: impact of 9/11 on children at risk for anxiety disorders.' *Journal of Anxiety Disorders 21*, 888–902.

Parker, G. and Manicavasagar, V. (1986) 'Childhood bereavement circumstances associated with adult depression.' *British Journal of Medical Psychology 59*, 387–391.

Parkes, C.M., Laungani, P. and Young, B. (1997) *Death and Bereavement. Across Cultures.* London: Routledge.

Parkes, C.M. and Weiss, R.S. (1983) *Recovery from Bereavement.* New York, NY: Basic Books.

Pennebaker, J.W. (1997) *Opening Up: The Healing Power of Expressing Emotions*, revised edition. New York, NY: Guilford Press.

Pfeffer, C.R., Altemus, M., Heo, M. and Jiang, H. (2007) 'Salivary Cortisol and psychopathology in children bereaved by the September 11, 2001 terror attacks.' *Biological Psychiatry 61*, 957–965.

Pfeffer, C., Karus, D., Siegel, K. and Jiang, H. (2000) 'Child survivors of parental death from cancer or suicide: depressive and behavioral outcomes.' *Psycho-oncology 9*, 1–10.

Poijula, S., Wahlberg, K.E. and Dyregrov, A. (2001a) 'Adolescent suicide and suicide contagion in three secondary schools.' *International Journal of Emergency Mental Health 3*, 169–175.

Poijula, S., Dyregrov, A., Wahlberg, K.E. and Jokelainen, J. (2001b) 'Reactions to adolescent suicide and crisis intervention in three secondary schools.' *International Journal of Emergency Mental Health 3*, 97–106.

Prigerson, H.G., Vanderwerker, L.C. and Maciejewski, P.K. (in press) 'Prolonged grief disorder: a case for inclusion in DSM-V.' In M. Stroebe, R. Hansson, H., Schut and W. Stroebe (eds). *Handbook of Bereavement and Practice: 21st Century Perspectives.* Washington, DC: American Psychological Association Press.

Pynoos, R.S. and Eth, S. (1984) 'The child as witness to homicide.' *Journal of Social Issues 40*, 87–108.

Rando, T.A. (1984) *Grief, Dying, and Death.* Champaign, IL: Research Press Company.

Rando, T.A. (1985) 'Creating therapeutic rituals in the psychotherapy of the bereaved.' *Psychotherapy 22*, 236–240.

Rando, T.A. (1986) *Parental Loss of a Child.* Champaign, IL: Research Press Company.

Rando, T.A. (1988) *Grieving: How to Go on Living when Someone You Love Dies.* Lexington, MA: Lexington Books.

Raundalen, M. (1989) *Ansvar och oppror.* Stockholm: Radda Barnens skrift-serie.

Raundalen, M. (2000) 'Hva skal vi si til barn om selvmord?' *Suicidiologi 5*, 12–15. Text available at: www.krisepsyk.no (accessed on 11 January 2008).

Raundalen, M., Lorentzen, G. and Dyregrov, A. (2005) *Gruppearbeid i flyktningfamilier.* Oslo: Pedagogisk forum.

Raveis, V.H., Siegel, K. and Karus, D. (1999) 'Children's psychological distress following the death of a parent.' *Journal of Youth and Adolescence 28*, 165–180.

Reinherz, H.Z., Giaconia, R.M., Hauf, A.M.C., Wasserman, M.S. and Silverman, A.B. (1999) 'Major depression in the transition to adulthood: risks and impairments.' *Journal of Abnormal Psychology 108*, 500–510.

Riches, G. and Dawson, P. (2000) 'Daughters' dilemmas: grief resolution in girls whose widowed fathers remarry early.' *Journal of Family Therapy 22*, 360–374.

Rosenblatt, P.C. (2000) *Parent Grief: Narratives of Loss and Relationship.* Philadelphia, PA: Brunner/Mazel.

Rothschild, B. and Rand, M. (2006) *Help for the Helper, Self-care Strategies for Managing Burnout and Stress.* New York, NY: W.W. Norton & Company.

Saigh, P.A., Yasik, A.E., Oberfield, R.A., Halamandris, P.V. and Bremner, J.D. (2006) 'The intellectual performance of traumatized children and adolescents with or without posttraumatic stress disorder.' *Journal of Abnormal Psychology 115*, 332–340.

Saldinger, A., Cain, A. and Porterfield, K. (2003) 'Managing traumatic stress in children anticipating parental death.' *Psychiatry 66*, 168–181.

Saler, L. and Skolnick, N. (1992) 'Childhood parental death and depression in adulthood: roles of surviving parent and family environment.' *American Journal of Orthopsychiatry 62*, 504–516.

Salmon, K. and Bryant, R.A. (2002) 'Posttraumatic stress disorder in children: the influence of developmental factors.' *Clinical Psychological Review 22*, 163–188.

Saylor, C.F. (Ed.). (1993) *Children and Disasters.* New York, NY: Plenum Press.

Saylor, C.F., Cowart, B.L., Lipovsky, J.A. and Finch jr., A.J. (2003) 'Media exposure to September 11.' *American Behavioral Scientist 12*, 1622–1642.

Siegel, K., Karus, D. and Raveis, V.H. (1996) 'Adjustment of children facing the death of a parent due to cancer.' *Journal of the American Academy of Child and Adolescent Psychiatry 35*, 442–450.

Silk, J.S., Shaw, D.S., Skuban, E.M., Oland, A.A. and Kovacs, M. (2006) 'Emotion regulation strategies in offspring of childhood-onset depressed mothers.' *Journal of Child Psychology and Psychiatry 47*, 69–78.

Silverman, P.R. and Worden, J.W. (1992) 'Children's reactions to the death of a parent in the early months after the death.' *American Journal of Orthopsychiatry 62*, 93–104.

Slaughter, V. (2005) 'Young children's understanding of death.' *Australian Psychologist 40*, 179–186.

Stamm, B.H. (ed.) (1995) *Secondary Traumatic Stress.* Lutherville, MD: Sidran Press.

Stoppelbein, L.A. and Greening, L. (2000) 'Posttraumatic stress symptoms in parentally bereaved children and adolescents.' *Journal of the American Academy of Child and Adolescent Psychiatry 39*, 1112–1119.

Stroebe, M. and Schut, H. (2006) 'To continue or relinquish bonds: a review of consequences for the bereaved.' *Death Studies 29*, 477–494.

Stroebe, M., Schut, H. and Stroebe, W. (2005) 'Attachment in coping with bereavement. A theoretical integration.' *Review of General Psychology 9*, 48–66.

Stroebe, M.S., Stroebe, W. and Hansson, R.O. (1993) *Handbook of Bereavement. Theory, Research, and Intervention.* New York, NY: Cambridge University Press.

Tein, J.Y., Sandler, I.N. and Ayers, T.S. (2006) 'Mediation of the effects of the family bereavement program on mental health problems of bereaved children and adolescents.' *Prevention Science 7*, 179–195.

Terr, L. (1979) 'Children of Chowchilla: a study of psychic trauma.' *Psychoanalytic study of the child 34*, 547–623.

Terr, L. (1983) 'Chowchilla revisited: the effects of psychic trauma four years after a school-bus kidnapping.' *American Journal of Psychiatry 140*, 1543-1550.

Toubiana, Y.H., Milgram, N.A., Strich, Y. and Edelstein, A. (1988) 'Crisis intervention in a school community disaster: principles and practices.' *Journal of Community Psychology 16*, 228–240.

Valente, S.M., Saunders, J. and Street, R. (1988) 'Adolescent bereavement following suicide: an examination of relevant literature.' *Journal of Counseling and Development 67*, 174–177.

Weller, R.A., Weller, E.B., Fristad, M.A. and Bowes, J.M. (1991) 'Depression in recently bereaved prepubertal children.' *American Journal of Psychiatry 148*, 1536–1540.

Worden, J.W. (1996) *Children and Grief.* New York, NY: Guilford Press.

Worden, J.W. and Silverman, P.R. (1996) 'Parental death and the adjustment of school-age children.' *Omega: Journal of Death and Dying 33*, 91–102.

Yule, W. and Gold, A. (1993) *Wise Before the Event. Coping with Crises in Schools.* London: Calouste Gulbenkian Foundation.

Yule, W. and Williams, R.M. (1990) 'Post-traumatic stress reactions in children.' *Journal of Traumatic Stress 3*, 279–295.

Zambelli, G.C., Clark, E.J., Barile, L. and deJong, A.F. (1988) 'An interdisciplinary approach to clinical intervention for childhood bereavement.' *Death Studies 12*, 41–50.

Index

GRIEF IN YOUNG CHILDREN

A HANDBOOK FOR ADULTS

ATLE DYREGROV

96 pages ISBN 978 1 84310 650 0 pb

Praise for the author:

> 'Dyregrov's writing is clear in its description, and explicit in its advice, and demonstrates that the daunting task of helping a child through grief is both manageable and rewarding'
>
> *– Bereavement Care*

Preschool children experience grief in the same way that older children do, but are often overlooked or neglected because they do not express grief in the same way.

Grief in Young Children provides parents and carers with all the information they need to develop a good understanding of loss in the early years. Illustrated throughout with case examples, bereavement expert Atle Dyregrov explores young children's reactions to death and loss, both immediately after the event and over time. For example, young children may engage in 'magic thinking' – believing that wishing someone dead can actually cause death – which often leads to feelings of guilt. Full of practical advice on issues such as how to remember the person, how to answer difficult questions and suggestions for exploring feelings through play, this accessible book enables adults to help children to develop an acceptance of grief and an understanding of death and loss.

This book is essential reading for parents, carers, counsellors and teachers.

Contents: Foreword 1. What is grief? 2. What can be done to help children who have suffered a loss? 3. Children's participation in rituals. 4. How do children process what has happened over time? 5. Supporting children over time. 6. Summary of advice to parents. 7. Specific advice. 8. Conclusion. Resources. Bibliography. Index.

Order this book online now via our website: www.jkp.com.